THE OTHER HALF OF THE
$\mathcal{R}$*AINBOW*

VERA WATERS

*PENN
COTTAGE
BOOKS*

ISBN 0 9516952 1 5

A CIP record for this book is available from the British Library.

Published by Penn Cottage Books, Ground Floor, Prudential Buildings, 79 Union Street, Oldham OL1 1HL, England. Telephone: 0161 627 4327

Elements of this book appeared in Vera Waters' first book, *Half a Rainbow,* and have been included here to fit in with what the author is trying to achieve. *Billy* was first published in the *Nursing Times*.

Front cover drawing by Leonard Varley

Cover design by Dawn Brend

Typeset by Paul Hanks

Printed and bound by
Whitstable Litho Printers Ltd., Whitstable, Kent.

And it shall come to pass,
when I bring a cloud over the earth,
that the bow shall be seen in the cloud

Genesis 9

Acknowledgements

My grateful thanks to the following people:

My agent John Gammons who made sure I continued to write, then firmly insisted I met deadlines

My secretary Bernie who worked on the manuscript until her head swam

Leonard Varley for permission to use his cover drawing again

Harry Wright for his photography

Steve Rigg for his suggestion of the title

The families of those people mentioned in "On Being Extra ... ordinary" who gave me permission to write of those they love

Ann my friend for always being there, together with Barbara and Rosey

Sister Mary John and the nuns at the Bernadine Priory, Warton, who pray for me and those I seek to help

Noel and Mary, my friends in Malta whose caring empathy encourages me to continue writing

Kath and Frank, my dear friends in Yorkshire whose support whilst writing this book has been invaluable

To everyone whose story is told or referred to and especially to those people not mentioned here who helped me while I was compiling the book

And, finally, my daughter Izzy whose love and quiet wisdom warms my heart when I feel cold

Preface

Completing my first book "Half a Rainbow" was to me like giving birth to a child. Painful yet rewarding. I hoped that the book would not only be of interest to its readers but also that it would provide help and support. Many letters and telephone calls proved to me that my words and stories did help. Now my second book is complete and my hopes are just as before. If you as an individual gain one tiny iota of comfort or help from reading "The Other Half of the Rainbow" then all the work and effort has been worthwhile. It isn't my intention to give instruction or heavy advice, merely to provide you with food for thought through the true stories and experiences not only of other people but also myself.

Life is full of stories and happenings, but nothing in life's experience can really be new for there is no guarantee that whatever has happened in your life has not happened in the life of another.

Often when I have completed a talk or lecture, members of the audience tell me that what I have said is really just about common sense. The drawback with common sense is that good sense is far from common. If this were not so, then we would learn nothing from other people's life experiences. When I was a girl I became interested in patchwork. The joining and mingling of so many tiny pieces of fabric intrigued me. It seemed unbelievable that so many pieces could form a whole, larger piece of cloth. Light, bright, dull, dark pieces joined at each seam. A

1

memory quilt with each piece evoking a precious picture in the mind.

A scrap from a bridesmaid's dress

A piece from a father's shirt

Another scrap from a linen table cloth

A piece cut from broad satin ribbon

A scrap of lining from a loving mother's coat

A piece of brocade which once adorned a bay window

Each piece with a story to tell.

My fascination with patchwork grew and when I read that the flags carried in the Crusades were really made of patches sewn together, I began to appreciate that life itself is really a patchwork.

Each segment and part of our existence is yet another scrap in the quilt of our life span. Every death and bereavement we feel is a dull little hexagon whilst every happy golden day provides a brightly coloured part of the whole and so the many patches of our life experience are joined together. When the multi coloured quilt is finished there is a need for someone to line and neaten all the edges, to provide a covering for all the joins betwixt one piece and another. Could it be that love and friendship, belief and faith in God are the lining to life's quilt?

This book contains many life patches, small stories told of people's endeavours and their experiences. If as you read you hear yourself saying "I've done just that" then be thankful. If as you read your eyes become moist and you are reminded of someone you love then again be thankful. If as you read you find yourself making promises that you intend to keep, then once more be thankful — oh and if as you read you find yourself smiling or laughing then take the pleasure of that emotion and enjoy it to the full.

In this patchwork quilt of life there is much to be learned. My family are now grown. Once I was talking to them about my death and afterwards. One of my sons said that he imagined the day when they would all be in the crematorium as my coffin disappeared behind the purple curtain. He said he could see that what might well happen would be that just at the final moment my voice would be heard saying "we seem to have a bit of a problem here!"

For those of you who have never met me, you may need to re-read this little snippet when you have read the book. For those who know what my philosophy of life is really about then you will understand immediately. My life has been spent counselling others. I feel I only continue to be fit to do exactly that whilst I remember that I myself could be tomorrow's client, for I have no idea what life will throw at me, what pitfalls there may be in my path, what mountains I might have to climb. I do not know if I will cope therefore, counsellor though I am, I could be tomorrow's client. I have always endeavoured to encourage my family, friends and clients to "seize the day."

Embracing life and death in that order, as you read I am with you in spirit, hoping that you gain some solace and comfort but most of all hope from these pages.

As for me my search for rainbows continues. A hint of sunshine in a rainy sky and I am out of the house or stopping the car to stare up into the sky. Then looking from left to right I seek the bow. Do you? Oh and if by some wonderful lucky chance I see one, a feeling of immeasurable joy courses through my veins and I feel like a new person. I don't know about Noah but if my feelings are anything to go by then when God placed his promised bow in the sky Noah must have felt reassured and elated.

Yes, I know the scientific explanation for rainbows but explain this if you can. On the very day that my first book was launched exactly half a rainbow could be seen in the sky . . .

Our greatest glory is not in
never falling, but in rising
every time we fall.

Confucius (551–479 BC)

Confidence

Are you a confident person? Do you appear to others confident as you face life with its various complications and crises? Do you give the impression of having a calm presence or is it all really an act?

Often people who consider themselves to be lacking in confidence envy those who appear to have this so called gift. The same people use phrases like "oh I wish I was like you. I wish I could talk to people. I wish I knew what to say". And so they go on. Recently completing a course with mature students I gave each of them a present. Thay had passed through a demanding self awareness workshop which meant that they had had to constantly appraise themselves — their faults, their shortcoming, their talents and their gifts. The gift I gave them was a small wooden box, inlaid on the lid with a brass duck. They opened their gifts and then smiled. It was not necessary for me to explain that the short but intense course of training had been designed not to make them totally confident to the level of arrogance, but to enable them to become people who like the duck on the surface appear to be floating along whilst underneath in the water they paddle like fury.

For me ducks are significant. It had not been my aim during the workshop to produce swans, that level of confidence comes at a much later date. We laughed together and each one went away with their reminder.

Confidence is about learning the skill of understanding yourself, after all it is difficult for someone else to have confidence in us if we are not confident in ourselves. Often we spend many worrying hours thinking anxiously about what other people will think. A good way of getting it all into perspective is to ask yourself the following questions:-

a. How many people do I know who would give me a kidney if I needed one?

b. How many people would pay all my debts, my mortgage, my rent etc. simply because I asked them to?

c. How many people do I sleep with?

"Sleep with?" I hear you say. Yes that's what I said, sleep with. You see, if we want the true answers to these questions we have to come a lot nearer to home than mere friends and acquaintances and people who might see us in our less confident state. Because, of course, it is those we love who would give us a kidney, those who love us who would help us to pay our debts and sometimes we actually sleep with the people whom we love. Surely these are the only people we should really worry about? Families, close friends.

A good measure of friendship is to ask yourself how many of your friends could you ring in the night and merely say "please come" without that person saying why, what, where and when. In other words a friend who is activated merely by the sound of your voice. A friend who doesn't ask questions, is motivated only by love and affection and will come to your help. It isn't usually those people who we worry about with regard to our confidence. In most instances we are more confident with them than the strangers we meet elsewhere, the colleagues we know at work, the acquaintances who we will never possibly meet again. Yet this is what confidence is about — "what will those people think about me?" So often we give such

7

importance to people who really do not have an important role to play in our lives.

If you want to really do something about the level of your confidence then try a little experiment. Sit in a pub or cafe, crowded place, hotel, wherever it might be and eavesdrop on conversations. You will find it amazing how many sentences you hear that start with "I told my mother the other day", "I knew what I was talking about", "my boss thought", I and my, so little about the other person. Do you really think that the majority of people who are self centred enough to start so many of their sentences with "I" or to talk about themselves at length are really interested in what you are about and what level of confidence you have? Be assured this is definitely not the case.

So there we have it, lack of confidence is about worrying what other people will think about us, people who have no real value in our lives. What do we do about it? First of all we set about liking the person we are, the person who lives in the mirror is definitely us. Many people dislike a certain part of their anatomy, that is why recently a group of people having their photographs taken were holding in their stomachs wanting to look right. Nothing wrong in that, age sometimes brings about portliness and there is nothing inappropriate about wanting to look our best, but it is important to like the person you are instead of worrying about the person you might be.

It is quite natural to worry about the level of confidence if we are in the early stages of a relationship, especially if the relationship is with a person whom we already believe ourselves to be in love with. That is a whole different kettle of fish, because then we worry about the way we present ourselves simply because we want that person to like us. Could it be that this is where confidence starts or indeed where it is lacking, that we lack confidence because we so desperately wish to be liked by others? There may be people who do not particularly like us. The average man or woman is not loved passionately by every person with whom he or she comes into contact, that would not be natural or normal. However it is true to say that if you have a quiet assurance about yourself and a calmness then you will create a response in others which is much more likely to build your confidence as it builds theirs.

There are some people whom we meet who give us an instant sense of being. People who make us feel good by simply being with us. You too could be a person like that but in order to be that sort of person, to have that affect on others, you must be quietly at peace with yourself. Being at peace with yourself is having a level of confidence which, far removed from arrogance, has with it almost a sense of humility, a humbleness which means that the person accepts what they are. Aspiring to greater things can be extremely healthy but if that aspiration causes the person to be arrogant and bombastic then nothing has been achieved.

If you feel you are under confident look again in the mirror, ask yourself a few simple facts about the person you are:

a. What is my favourite colour?
b. What is my favourite piece of clothing?
c. What is my favourite fruit?
d. What is my favourite animal?

e. What is my favourite drink?
f. What is my favourite food?
g. What kind of weather do I like most?
and last but by no means least — when do I feel I look
my best?

One of my clients went through each of these
questions and then looked at me and said "I suppose I
look at my best when I am in my fluffy bathrobe with
my hair wrapped in a towel with my furry mules on my
feet." She then laughed heartily. "It's true" she said,
"I like myself then because I feel cosy and warm and
often I curl up in front of the fire and watch the
television and feel I can just be myself." She had it in a
nutshell didn't she? It's about feeling yourself. You
need to know about yourself to be confident, to know
exactly what kind of a person you are. You could say
what silly questions, of course I know my favourite
colour but take it further, find out more. Ask yourself
what kind of a person you really are. What do other
people see, what do you want them to see?

The other day one of my granddaughters returned
from school. She is four years of age and on her
cardigan was a stick-on label on which the teacher had
drawn a smiley face. She was very proud of this little
face. That evening one of my grandsons telephoned to
tell me that it had been his first day at school and he
too had a smiley face on his jumper. Simple really —
just labels, labels that shopkeepers stick upon articles
telling us how much they are but somebody somewhere with a little magic inside them has come up with
the idea of a smiley face on a round stick on label. Both
of these children are learning about confidence. They
are learning that it is a good thing to have a smiley face
on your jumper because then other people ask

what the smiley face means. Confidence, where does it begin?

Oh I can hear you saying not so, not so, what if I look a fool, what if people laugh at me? So what, what does it matter if the whole world laughs but you are sure that at the end of it all you like you. That person who lives in your mirror is the person whom you should respect more than anyone else in the world for if you do not respect yourself how can anyone else? Loving and respecting yourself is one of the first lessons to be learned as we think about being confident. It is no use to say I can't, far more truthful to say I won't, I am afraid, I don't know how.

No one is suggesting being confident is easy. Sometimes I get quite cross with people who think that because of my work I can cope with anything. Once when I was speaking publicly a woman in the audience during the question time said she knew that people like me didn't have problems in their own homes. Luckily for me some people in the audience thought her comments rather silly. I looked at her and thought of the absolute chaos I had left behind that morning. There on the stage I was trying very hard to look serene on the surface but believe me I was paddling like fury underneath, just another duck-like human swimming on the lake of life!

Nothing at that time in my life was going right. I didn't know where to start. I believed that the whole world could see that I lacked confidence. It wasn't true because you see that women standing there believed that by virtue of what I do I couldn't have problems like her. I tried to speak to her afterwards but no matter what I said she didn't want to know the Vera

Waters who might have something in common with her. She didn't want to know the person I sometimes am when things get on top of me. I don't appear to be very confident then.

Often so called confident people have much deeper troughs than those who are less confident because acting confidently takes a lot of time and effort. Ask yourself why so many comedians, actors, people in the public eye actually go off and quietly break down. Double lives. Something else inside, something different on the outside.

We learn about confidence in our early years. Recently a couple came to see me with a young child, a boy of four. During the course of the time we spent together, the parents and I, I asked them if they respected him. They said they loved him. I repeated my question "do you respect him?" "He is only four" said the father. "Do you respect him?" "He wouldn't understand" said the mother. It wasn't the child who had the problem it was the parents.

As children we need to know that we are really valued and made to feel special. That is where most people first learn about confidence. The child who is praised will have some confidence. The child who knows where the boundaries are will gain confidence daily because he learns the rules of staying within those boundaries and being praised for doing so. Some children are deprived of this wonderful learning part of their young lives. For them the journey to confidence is much harder. They must take the painful stone strewn road that the luckier child does not have to tread. For these children who grow into adults confidence is gained bit by painful bit until at last they believe in themselves, because somewhere along the way their parents did not love and respect them enough to give them the confidence to get on in life.

Are you a confident person? Do you appear to others confident as you face life with its various complications and crises? Do you give the impression of having a calm presence, or is it really an act? Often people who consider themselves to be under confident envy those who appear to have this so called gift. They do not necessarily want to appreciate that most people have to work hard at being confident.

If I were asked to give what I consider the single most useful bit of advice for all humanity it would be this: expect trouble as an inevitable part of life and when it comes hold your head high, look it squarely in the eye and say "I will be bigger than you. You cannot defeat me."

Ann Landers, 1918

Each new generation that comes
takes one look at the world,
thinks wildly,
"Is this all they've done to it?"
and bursts into tears.

Clarence Day, The Crow's Nest, 1921

Babies

The other day we had a christening in the family. One of my granddaughters. She is a very pleasant little baby who appears to enjoy life. She smiles almost all the time and when prompted will giggle deliciously with passers by. It was to be her big day, the day for going to church and letting God into her life. However for her it did not feel like a big day. She had been ill the evening before and obviously was out of sorts with the world. It was a joint christening with another family. Their child serene and peaceful, isn't it always the case? Our family baby so unlike herself cried for the whole of the ceremony. However, the priest as he was about to start touched her gently and asked if she would mind if he started the ceremony. Momentarily she stopped her noise.

Just for a moment try to imagine how a baby sees the world. Here was little Beth dressed up in a long white gown, not used to wearing long white dresses and petticoats, she felt ill at ease. But how can you as a baby explain to adults what is happening in your life when you gurgle and giggle and they speak another language. A language that you cannot speak but soon you realise that if you are to communicate with them at all, you must learn this foreign tongue. Why, thinks the baby, can't they speak as I speak, gurgling, making chortling noises? Is this not speech enough but, no, the baby must learn to speak properly in order to be understood.

So the day continued for Beth until with relief we

removed her dress, gave her her welcome bottle and she peaceably slept. You can imagine her wondering what all the fuss was about.

The baptismal candle stands on the mantelpiece to remind her of the day she was baptised. Do you remember your baptismal day, do any of us remember? We are regaled with stories of our behaviour at the font. "The Vicar nearly dropped you" we hear someone say. "You screamed all the time", but the baby has no point of response.

Have you ever wondered what it feels like to be a baby? Newly born into the world you are placed in a cot by your mother's bed. It is hospital white and hygienic. Suddenly there is noise, a lot of noise, what is that noise, you are later to learn it is the sound of your grandmother laughing, it sounds like nothing you have ever heard in your short life before and then there is a swoosh of air as you are picked up. You find yourself surrounded by space. Then suddenly clutched towards a rough place your cheek feels chaffed, you are not to know at that time that this is your father's tweed jacket. Then as if this is not enough, you find yourself literally sailing through space as you are passed from person to person, and you ache and long for the warm nest of the womb from which you came. Here the nightmare does not end and you make the only sound you know about, you cry, you are so surprised at the sound that comes from yourself, that you are afraid and you cry even more.

You hear these people around you saying "Oh dear he's crying" or "Does he need feeding?" "Does he need his nappy changing?" and so it goes on. Surely the baby must want to say "I came from a warm dark cosy place, I am no longer in that warm dark cosy place, I am in another place that I do not particularly like, please let me sleep, let me rest, let me snuggle next to the body of the person who brought me here for she and only she is my mummy."

Imagine three months later lying in your pram asleep. You have learned a lot in the three months, you can make noises, there is a nice face that comes near you, in fact there are a few nice faces but on this particular morning you awaken you are in your pram but the space through which the sunlight should come is blocked by three big faces whom you do not recognise. Something is touching your cheek and pulling at it and a voice is saying "coochy, coochy", words you do not understand, and also you do not like the feel of the finger nor the look on the face. You cry. The heads draw back and suddenly there is the face of the person you love most — mummy. She settles you down, strokes the cheek and once more you are content. Mummy, mummy please defend me from these marauding well wishers!

We all know that tiny babies cannot speak nor can they indicate to us positively how they feel. The next time you see someone holding a small baby aloft saying "whose a cheeky girl then" or even throwing the baby a few inches into the air, try a little empathy with the child. (Think shame, shame!). I am sure that many babies, if they could speak, would indicate some preferences about the way they are treated by the grown up beings in their world!

If a child lives with security
He learns to have faith
If a child lives with approval
He learns to like himself.

Christian Art Ltd.

The Child's Eye View

The top of the mantelpiece glistened in the sunlight and although the day was warm a fire burned in the grate. The door at the side of the fire had a bright large shiny knob and a lady bowed at my feet. She wore a strange bracelet full of spiky little heads and I can remember a yellow soft glow about my body. Touching the yellow glow I felt good and whole.

This is my first memory, the first picture that my mind recorded that could be easily retrieved. After many questions and answers I discovered that I was describing a fitting I had had for a new yellow muslin dress. At that time I was two and a half years old. Of course the lady's spiky bracelet was the pad of pins attached with a piece of elastic around her wrist and of course she was not bowing to me but bending her head as she pinned together the pieces of my dress whilst I stood high up on what seemed like the top of the mountain, the mountain being her kitchen table.

My memories are vivid and clear, being full of colour whether bright or at other times dark colours full of foreboding. These are the pictures of my past.

Try sitting quietly in your favourite chair, let a piece of music play in the background, sitting there you can start the journey. Travel back and discover for yourself where your life of memories began. If you find that the first recall you can summon is at the age of 10 or 12 or later then sit and sit and trawl again for there will be some memories there, good, bad, indifferent. It is only when you can recall those memories of your own that you can begin to understand how children really feel and react to life. Of course this is a different age, a different generation, a whole new world now but still a child's reactions are basic to that child and the only way to understand the child is to understand the child that was once yourself.

Imagine a little boy returning from school. The childminder has collected him but in order to reach her house they have to pass his own. Strange happenings at my house he thinks. A sign in the garden. A sign just like the one in the garden of the house on the corner, a sign that says 'For Sale'. Where are we going he asks himself. The childminder looks frustrated and goes pink when he asks her what it all means.

"Your Dad will explain" she says "when he comes to collect you." The waiting for this small boy is endless, from 3.30 to 7.00pm he must wonder what is happening in his life. No one loved or confided in him enough to involve him in this situation. His parents had made the decision to move, never thinking of the anguish he would feel at finding a 'For Sale' notice outside his house, the house in which he has his bedroom in which he keeps his precious toys and his little treasures.

No, I am not for one moment suggesting that you ask tiny children their opinions in matters of great importance for of course a small child may not understand. However, to warn him of what is happening puts him confidently in the picture. A man once said to me "we only told the twins two days before we moved because we didn't want to worry them." The twins as he collectively called them had known for months simply by following the clues. No 'For sale' sign in their garden but the constant tidying up and boxing away of their toys, to say nothing of the contents of the garage told them its own story. Why oh why do so many adults presume that children simply do not understand what is happening in their lives.

Even a small child is capable of understanding and in the absence of any explanation will, more often than not, put in place guessed information of their own. Often this information is totally incorrect. With "fobbing off" comments from the adults in their life they struggle to discover what is actually happening. Just like the boy who said after his father and mother had parted "well, my mum and dad didn't speak together for a long time". "Not so" yelled his mother, "he couldn't have known" she said, turning to me. "Well" said her young son "you put his pyjamas in the big bed every morning and made the little bed up to look tidy before I got up every morning." Incredulously his mother stared in silence. How did he know? At seven she didn't realise he had made it his business to know what was going on in his own house. He was tired of the sound of raised voices as he went to sleep. The banging in the night, the slamming of doors and the perceived front of hypocrisy in the morning.

Children who are given ongoing information about happenings in their lives cope much better. It is for instance always difficult to know whether to tell a child that one of their parents is dying. If the death seems to be some way off then small words of preparation need to form themselves so that the child learns lessons about the fact that not everything or anything lives forever. With a lot of love this awful information can be passed on to the child, assimilated and later acted upon.

If you gather together a group of six and seven year olds, win their confidence and talk to them intimately about the happenings in their lives. They will give you information that will increase the depth of your wisdom to such a degree that you will wonder how you had existed in life without it. The small boy who says "when my mother says we'll see, I know its never going to happen, when my daddy says one day, that's a non event as well." Children are not easily fobbed off but they are often given a double or dual morality. Take for instance the situation in which often we place them without realising, that we are placing upon them two different standards of behaviour.

Take an ordinary family; mum and dad, caring, working hard, wanting their children to grow up with honesty and integrity. There are rules of the house and home, there are rules regarding behaviour and the way in which they speak to one another but one rule prevails, that of truth, so mother says "we will not have any lies or untruths here" and children live by that code. In all too short a time those same children realise that this code does not exist for their parents, it exists only for them and as one boy put it "it's because you only have to do those things when you are little and not when you are grown up." I am referring of course to our natural hypocrisy when dealing with other people. Tea time for this family sitting round the table, conversation as follows:-

Mother: "You will never guess what happened at the Carter's today. A man came and took away quite a lot of furniture, looked like the bailiffs to me but then of course we know how much money she owes everybody."

Father grunts "well things have been difficult for them."

Mother: "That's no excuse, she owes everybody in the street and I'll bet she owes more money on her clubs than anyone else."

The children, ears like windmills, take in this information and inwardly digest — so the Carters up the road owe money. Judging from the conversation around the tea table the Carters are not liked by mum and dad. In fact, as the conversation continues it becomes more than evident that they are distinctly disliked.

Now children can cope with this because they have friends whom they dislike for no apparent reason. They in their kindness give the same licence to their adult counterparts but then how do they cope when the scene continues with a knock at the door, the door opening and Mr. Carter on the doorstep saying "I wonder if I can come in and have a word." False smiles all round, oh come in, come in. The children sit at the tea table quite baffled, here is Mr. Carter who father and mother have spent the last half hour criticising and he is in their house and now he is being offered a cup of tea, offered a cup of tea by two people whom these children respect, who they know dislike Mr. Carter intensely. The children in the family are faced with a dual morality, they have nowhere to go with it but they learn from it and they become aware that it is quite all right to be nice to someone's face and critical to them behind their back. The parents have forgotten the maxim which should prevail which says "if you can say nothing good, say nothing at all."

When I was a child this situation regarding parents and adults was brought home to me in rather a curious way and I can only hope that in later years the lady and gentleman involved forgave me for my tremendous *faux pas.*

I had heard my mother and father talking together about a woman who was a neighbour of ours further up the street. I heard them refer to a friend of hers whose name was Bernard as her fancy man who was never away. Later that day when walking up the street I saw Bernard in the garden of the lady neighbour. He was helping her to weed her herbaceous border. I climbed on to the garden gate and looked over at them both. They smiled and waved. I liked Bernard, I thought he had very kind eyes. I looked at him for a long time trying to decide what part of him was fancy. His shoes were just plain brown and his long sleeved shirt which he had rolled up to the elbows was just like those that my father wore. His trousers weren't particularly fancy either but then perhaps my father and mother were referring to his braces because they were a little fancy but not enough I thought for him to be called "a fancy man."

Mrs. Leeming went into the house and brought out two large glasses of lemonade and a smaller glass for me. "Come in Vera" she said, "don't stand on the outside of the gate, come in and sit down on the grass and have a drink with us." It was in those days when such invitations could be trusted, where there was no marauding evil to be perceived. I drank my lemonade and continued to survey Bernard until at last he asked me if there was anything the matter. I said "No." "What are you thinking?" he asked. "I am trying to decide how fancy you are." Mrs. Leeming looked at me "what do you mean Vera, fancy?" "Well" I said "my mum and dad said Bernard is your fancy man and I am trying to think which part of him is the most fancy." There was a deathly silence. Their two pint glasses were placed upon the tray. They smiled sad little smiles at me and I realised that in some awful way I had hurt them but I had no idea why. I began to feel uneasy so I said my goodbyes and left the garden which suddenly didn't seem sunny and warm anymore. Later that night when I was ready for bed I said to my father and mother "I saw Bernard today with Mrs. Leeming." "Oh yes" said my father. "I told him you said he was a fancy man and that I was trying to see what you meant but only his braces were really fancy." Another deathly silence and then my father looked at me and said nothing and my mother told me I was the most stupid girl she had ever met in her entire life.

So the stupid eight year old went to bed with no notion as to what she had done or not done, other than the knowledge that in some way without her knowing she had caused sadness in the faces of two adults and anger and frustration in the faces of another two adults. There were no explanations and it was many years before I realised just what I had done. Please include your children. You are privileged that a child comes into your life and that you are allowed to care for that child, to give the child love and have love in return but the child needs information as much as love, information that will help him or her to feel secure. Scant information, incorrect information, gossipy information gives the wrong messages and innocent people including the child suffer as a result. So the next time you find that you are about to say of your child "he doesn't understand," ask yourself if it's you that doesn't understand how much he could understand. Now there's a daunting thought!

Imagine the scene. I will try to paint a picture in words for you. Recently while visiting friends in Malta an invitation was extended to share a typical Maltese Sunday. No Yorkshire pudding or Sunday roast but something very different yet enduringly comforting. The Maltese usually go to church on a Sunday as a family, even teenagers are expected to accompany their parents. After church the families meet together talking animatedly, gesticulating, laughing together. Much more touching here in this Mediterranean island, with inhibitions much less obvious. Some families then return to their homes but for the majority a meal out is the order of the day. Flocking to their favourite restaurants they eat together. Families joined by boyfriends, girlfriends and others.

Small children also have their place within the family and there's always a helping hand for the little ones. For in Malta children are valued though the moral code is strictly adhered to, respect for parents and an abundance of love is ever present. After the meal, a walk. All the family walking, tiny tots on sturdy plastic bikes, grandparents, parents, and children, all together for Sunday. A small boy holds his mother's hand as he walks along on a sea front pulling a car behind him on a string, a little girl with glasses pulls at her mummy's hand and asks about her shadow and why it is getting longer and longer. Parents here converse with children ensuring that they have a special place in the heart of the family. There is much talking and interest in the world of the child. Was this how we once were a decade ago, two, three decades past? Did we respect our children in that way then?

What has happened to so many people, and why has there been such a change in our society? Is it because we live more in the fast lane then ever before?

The little boy who still has time to pull a car behind him on a string will give comfort to many, his very action showing that there is time in life for the simpler things.

In Malta the drivers constantly honk their horns at one another, they wave and shout and in a traffic jam a cacophony of sound can be heard as driver after driver press their horns repeatedly. This is no road rage though, it is accepted here that this is how people express themselves. There is nothing vicious about their actions. They show their feelings of joy and friendliness whilst we within our culture often suppress ours. It is no accident that in Malta the cases of mental illness are less per head of the population than here and that certain other illnesses are not as prevalent. Letting off steam can in itself be comforting, the driver honking his horn in a non aggressive manner in Malta still has time to spend with his child and in the meantime he has given vent to his pent up feelings in company with his fellow countrymen.

*As in filling a vessel drop by
drop, there is at last a drop
which makes it run over: so in a
series of kindness there is at
last one which makes the heart
run over.*
James Boswell

Emotional Bank

In my first book 'Half a Rainbow' I wrote about the importance of our emotional banking system. For those readers who have not read the book a recap is necessary.

Imagine that as a baby you are given an emotional bank book. Every positive loving action or thought makes a deposit whilst all the negative, hurtful experiences of life constitute withdrawals. So our lives go on. Our bank balance fluctuates, going up and down and all too often we find ourselves emotionally 'in the red'. With this sort of banking it's important to remember that life has many rainy days and saving for them is a good idea. Just like an ordinary bank, where pounds saved may be used when income drops for some reason, than also deposits saved in our emotional bank come in very useful during the periods of our life when everything seems to go wrong and good luck appears to have deserted us. At these times we can look into our emotional bank and remember the positive deposits.

Many of these deposits are unusual, mainly because we are all very different, each of us being unique. The day spent happily with someone we love can make a huge deposit; praise from a parent, manager or a friend makes yet another. A beautiful piece of music enjoyed in quiet solace easily deposits for the classical music lover, whilst someone else will take immense pleasure from rocking and rolling!

Our deposits do not have to be large, but they do

need to be constant, varied and continual. The balance in our emotional bank makes the difference between being happy and being sad. Usually those people who rarely deposit have little saved and therefore they cannot make withdrawals when most in need.

Let's look a little more closely at emotional banking. About a half a mile from Manchester City Centre is a harsh rough area. No interesting shops, no prettily curtained windows, just roads and factories and many "Mend-anything" establishments. At least twice a week I drive through the area. When I was a child it was full of rows upon rows of small terraced houses. At that time very few of them would have boasted the luxury of a bathroom. It was the land of tin baths, back yards and door steps which seemed especially designed to seat the gossiping ladies of the day. From these houses many men caught buses to their beloved allotments.

An allotment can be a beautiful place. Flowers, plants and company. Not the company thrust upon us but company sought, desired and appreciated. What is it about an allotment that makes it a special place to be? The allotment keeper usually plants so many seeds that when the crucial pricking out stage is reached he or she has as many to give away or exchange as are to be kept for personal needs. The allotment keeper is sometimes competitive, needing the challenge of other gardeners and growers. Yet when they need to be, as Greta Garbo used to say, "alone" an allotment lends itself to this as well.

The true value of this wonderful place is found in the fact that grown adults can become almost invisible. Shouts of "have you seen my dad" echo across the plots, heads turn, faces smile, eyes respond. So often 'dad' remains elusive until appearing like the proverbial rabbit produced by the experienced magician. Oh the joy and value of an allotment! You will notice that as yet I have not said a word about produce. A mere aside for many! Allotmenteering like mountaineering makes huge deposits in the emotional bank. So as I drive through this barren waste I often think of the people who once lived there in the streets.

As this is the age of miracles they often come to us in the strangest places. A few days ago as I passed the mend-anything workshops I noticed what I had originally thought was a hedge of rough bushes. Bushes they were but no ordinary bushes. These bushes were brambles full to bursting with the largest blackberries I had ever seen let alone gathered. I stopped the car and began to look frantically for something to put these edible treasures in. Pouncing on a half empty tissue box on the back seat I hurriedly emptied its contents and locked the car. After all I was in a very bad area.

For the next 10 whole minutes I picked the fruit. In those precious fragments of the hour I filled my makeshift container. The sun was shining brightly, a few cars passed but for all intents and purposes I could have been miles away in the heart of the country. Oh, there were the city sounds and smells but for me I was encapsulated within my own enjoyment. On arriving home I weighed the berries. 2lb. At sometime in the past someone had allowed these bushes to bloom and blossom. Despite changes, not necessarily for the good, nature continued producing flowers which were then to become fruits. What a lot of emotional banking. My credit register rose dramatically.

When I reached the place where the berries were growing I had felt very angry. I had left a meeting where I had allowed someone to make me feel angry. A man I consider to be without light in his soul. A man who seemed to dwell in a world of black and white with no perception of grey or the colours of the rainbow. His total inflexibility had left me feeling emotionally drained and disabled. I had allowed this to happen to me. Then I saw the fruit and as I picked the large berries I no longer felt angry, just incredibly sorry for this colourless man. Try to bank emotionally every day of your life, make time no matter how weary you feel. Unless you keep your banking active you will pay a very high price as a consequence.

Banking our positive emotions such as happiness and fulfilment is about saving with the sure knowledge that a high rate of fixed interest will always be paid.

Vera Waters

*"If you have made mistakes . . .
there is always another chance
for you . . .
You may have a fresh start any
moment you choose, for this
thing we call 'failure' is not the
falling down, but the staying
down."*

Mary Pickford (1893–1979), Actress

Making Survival Easier

Sometime in our lives most of us get to a stage where we feel we are not coping very well. Stress may be an overused word, however there are times when we just don't know which way to turn. Those are the days when we feel as though everything is on top of us. One lady once described it as feeling as though she was in the bottom of the washing basket and someone had put all the washing in on top of her and she couldn't get out. She described the washing as not being very heavy and knew she wasn't suffocating, but try as she might she couldn't get out of the muddle she felt she was in. In order not only to survive but to get through these days when everything gets on top of us — and let's face it sometimes it's not days it's whole periods of our lives — then we need some strategies for coping. Often it's the very simplest solutions that have the most effect.

It may be that at the beginning of a particular day you face so many chores and things to do that you are overwhelmed before you begin. You start to use phrases like 'oh I'll never get through all of this' or 'how will I cope with this' or even worse 'there aren't enough hours in the day.' Take a small part out of that day, usually just a few minutes will do. Make a list. Oh I know it sounds rather silly, make a list, it takes time to make a list, it does, but while you are making it you are actually beginning to sort out and unravel the chaos of the day.

It is necessary to put on your list the simplest things you have to do even if these include picking the children up from school, doing the ironing, phoning the managing director, ringing husband at work, getting in touch with your wife, remembering there is no butter in the fridge, keeping in your mind the fact that you have too many things to do in too little time. Make the list anyway. If you include on it the small things then the list is much longer and you could say 'well that's even more daunting' but that's not so. It actually isn't more daunting. It's a longer list but there are some easy tasks on it that take a small amount of time and are much easier to accomplish. So put down washing up, making beds, driving to work, parking the car, list them all, the list will seem endless but then think of the achievement. As each job is done you can score it off.

Take the working person arriving at work, taking chaos in the car with you. You get there, you park the car, a bold line through that entry, you've dropped the children at school, another line, so it goes on. At home the washing's done, cross it out, shopping done, cross it out and so on and so forth. At the end of the day there will be items on that list, jobs you haven't done, tasks remaining incomplete, so take another sheet of paper and put tomorrow's date on it and transfer jobs left undone onto that list and get yourself ready for tomorrow. List making really does work. Many of the most methodical, efficient people in the world work by lists. The top executive learns not to be ashamed as he says "I need everything to be written down." Good secretaries produce lists of jobs that need to be done, meetings to attend, clients to see, but the crossing off of those jobs brings satisfaction to the person who has to do them.

If you are trying to teach a small child what achievement is about and the child is struggling, then lists work with children just as much as they work with adults. Give a child a big fat coloured crayon, write down all the tasks — toys away, teeth to be cleaned, clothes to be folded, bedtime and let the child put the list on the wall. Every task completed the child crosses it out, 'look mummy, look daddy, I've done four things today.' It's all about achieving order out of chaos.

Order out of chaos is one of the best ways of coping with the stresses of everyday life. There are strategies that work in many different situations. Take, for instance, buying a house. Everyone knows that buying a house is a highly traumatic operation, as is selling one.

Let's look at buying a house. Imagine you are in the happy position of being almost sure of a sale on your property. If you haven't already started the search, you begin frantically to look for another house that will suit you and your family. It is so easy to bound into the estate agents and make arrangements to see several houses almost all at once, as though it were possible to view a few houses simultaneously. It's not the answer. Before you go make a list, how many bedrooms, kitchen, bathroom, do you need a utility room, yes, put it down, garage, oh yes I need a garage, garden, well doesn't everyone want a garden, gardens back and front, adequate parking, main road position, secluded, shower, bath, both, one with one toilet, rural or suburban, the list is endless but if you have a list which contains everything, all the points that you want your new home to have, then at least you will not waste time looking at properties that do not fit the bill.

You have to be strong though because along will come the estate agent who wants you to look at a property. He or she may know full well that it does not suit your requirements completely, but persuasion being the powerful game it is, you may well find yourself looking longingly around the house that does not have garage space and yet you have a car. You then fall into a trap of wondering how you can cope with this problem, as though it was a shortcoming of your own in the first place. Remember, if you had not been coerced into viewing the property, then you wouldn't be in this process of indecision. Often it is not the doing that makes us feel at odds with ourselves or even the waiting, it's the indecision, that horrible limbo time when we can't make up our minds.

Of course you want to buy a new house, of course you could make that one do but for how long, you always wanted a garden and here you are in a property without one. Is it enough to say "well, the ceilings are high, the rooms are as big as I want." But you wanted a garden as well and the property which you have chosen does not have one. So that means that in many ways you cannot be truly content because you have allowed another person to decide what was best for you. Another person entered into the equation and often in the case of estate agents it is about having properties to sell. Properties for sale need buyers. Stick to your guns, you are the person who is going to live there, remember that you are entitled to have what you want, without being brow beaten into making the wrong choice.

Then there are doctor's surgeries. Look at the service provided by receptionists and see what actually happens to us as we enter these portals as patients. But the story starts much earlier than that doesn't it? It starts with the telephone call to make the appointment. "What is it for?" So many people when they hear the voice at the other end suddenly feel well. You are about to make an appointment and as the receptionist asks "can I help you", you find yourself thinking well perhaps I am not really ill. Then when she says "the doctor can't see you today or tomorrow or the day after" and offers you an appointment Friday next week suddenly you not only feel ill you feel angry. Many times we want to say "I'll be ill to order" but the receptionist has her job to do and in most instances she tries to look after the doctor's needs, as well as the patient's, and let's face it many people go to see their doctor when there is nothing wrong with them, filling a valuable slot of time which could be better spent by a doctor seeing a patient who is really in need.

If you need that appointment then again stand by what you want. If you don't you will be frustrated and really distressed during the rest of the day and probably pass on a lot of your anger and frustration to others. Stay with it.

"I need an appointment to see the doctor very soon."

"Sorry there are no appointments until next week."

This is an impasse isn't it, you want the appointment, it isn't an emergency, she says she hasn't got any. Have you ever tried saying "well if that's the case can you put me on the doctor's visiting list?" Amazingly this often works and then an abrupt voice will say your appointment is 5.30 tonight or 9.15 in the morning. Suddenly you have been fitted in to the doctor's already busy schedule and you wouldn't have been if you hadn't held your ground.

I was talking to a woman recently who said she

couldn't do any of that. It made her get too agitated. That lady has a choice as we all have between feeling agitated at what she manages to achieve and feeling frustrated at not achieving anything at all, but then you see the power of a receptionist comes from the fact that when we are patients we are momentarily turned into children. Bearing in mind that our personalities have three parts, the child, the parent and the adult, it is worth remembering that most times when we go to the hospital or the surgery it is the child in us that responds and we don't enter those places with confidence. We feel ill. Disadvantaged.

We go seeking not only information and expertise but Tender Loving Care. A touch of the old T.L.C. Not a lot of T.L.C. to be found in Out Patients in many hospitals, the nurse barks a name over her right shoulder, was that me, you turn to the people sitting next to you, none of them are laughing, after all they are patients. "Did you hear what name she called?" you ask. "Mather" oh, a sigh of relief, not me. If we want to go to the toilet, now there's a dilemma and the very thought of it can make us feel anxious and agitated. If I go to the toilet she might well call my name and I'll miss my appointment, what will I do, oh be blowed go to the toilet anyway and when you come out, go to the nurse and say "I've just been to the toilet did you by any chance call my name." She is not authorised to control you you know, she is there to do a job, to provide a service to patients, she is only too glad to let you know that it's not your turn yet, so you sit down. On one side of you is a man, noisily reading the paper, grunting as he goes along, to the other side a lady busily discussing her ailments and another woman speaking to you across from her. They then go into detail about which consultant they will be seeing, a further woman joins the conversation as does the man. They try desperately to upstage one another with their ailments. It's all very uplifting isn't it. This experience is not designed to make you feel better nor to make you feel positive.

It really isn't necessary to be verbally confrontational with people whom you meet, whether they be in authority or whether they believe that they are in an authoritarian situation and are therefore in control. It is important that you make your voice heard without shouting, that you make it clear to the listener that you will not be moved, nor coerced, nor bullied, but that you might be persuaded to understand their point of view if you are treated politely. All of this takes confidence. I can hear some people saying "I haven't that sort of confidence." Alright, but confidence is something that we can work at. We don't have to be so boringly confident that we actually make ourselves the sort of person who is difficult for others to be with. We can be quietly confident, ensuring that without offending other people we make it clear that we will not necessarily take no for an answer.

Patients in hospital are vulnerable from the word go. This is because when we are ill it suits the establishment to keep us in the child part of our personality, this is why on entering hospital we are often asked to take a bath. We know that we took a shower or a bath before we left the house but still we are asked to do just that.

We are given scant information. I remember once in a casualty department asking a nurse what she was injecting me with. She said "the doctor will tell you."

"I am asking you" I said. "The doctor will tell you", so I said "well I am sorry, I don't want the injection because by the time the doctor tells me I might decide I don't want it." She spat out the word "tetanus" oh, light dawned, I was informed. I then told her she could give me the injection.

There are many good, devoted medical nursing staff, the sort of people one would feel privileged to meet in a patient situation. Sadly they are often the most overworked and in many cases they outnumber those who use their position powerfully. Yes, nurses have a lot to put up with but so do patients. Well you could say what has all this got to do with life crises. Some of the worst situations we ever experience are in hospital. I for one am very glad that such places exist because in them are people who know far more about my body than I do, all I require is that they ask my permission about what they are going to do, and that provided I am conscious and composmentis I can discuss with them their intentions.

So now if we look back we have got making lists, being firmly but gently assertive, refusing to be coerced and somehow making a stand in a medical arena. If doing these things becomes part of your life then you will not feel so anxious, and you might actually like yourself a little bit more. After all there is nothing worse than having an incident in your life and finding yourself saying "I should have said this, if only I'd said the other, why didn't I think of that." Alright let it happen once or twice. Starting tomorrow look at things positively, decide that you are not going to have a lifetime of saying "I should have done it differently." Start tomorrow and do it differently. The only way to achieve this is to make sure that you have got the courage of your convictions. Stand by them. Oh dear, I can hear someone sighing, all the negative thoughts are coming back. Go on, try it anyway. You have nothing to lose and believe me it might just work.

"If you do things well, do them
better. Be daring, be first,
be different, be just."

Anita Roddick,
Founder and managing director,
Body Shop International

Those who bring sunshine to the lives of others cannot keep it from themselves

J. M. Barrie (1860–1937)

Embarrassment

Recently I watched a TV programme, it was all about that well known comedian Norman Wisdom. There he was on the screen, laughing one minute, crying the next. Nothing unusual in that you might think, because after all isn't that what he does on the stage and in his films all the time, but within ten minutes I felt very humbled by his disclosures.

He had had a very difficult childhood, and he described the way in which he remembered his father throwing him up into the air so hard that he hit the ceiling. Then he laughed, made a joke, said it had taught him how to fall. He spoke of his mother leaving and the way in which some years later she bought him a tricycle. His father seeing him riding the tricycle smashed it up completely. Norman Wisdom said, for all to hear, he just thought that was the way things were. Not very much in the way of deposits going into his emotional bank, in fact very little. Yet somehow he took all of that unhappiness, all the neglect, all the pain, all the hardship and instead of letting it burden him for the rest of his life so that he became bitter and cynical, he took it home and converted it into something quite different, namely humour. Could it be that we as human beings have finally arrived at stability when we can laugh at ourselves? Could it be that when the joke is on us and we can look at other people and laugh with them that we have finally achieved the achievable?

People talk to me about embarrassment, they tell me they can't do something because it's embarrassing. The woman who said to me that she couldn't tell her mother she loved her because it was a bit embarrassing, and it wasn't the sort of thing that was done in their family, made me think again about embarrassment.

When I was five years old, I attended a school which was quite a distance from my home. My mother would put me on the bus in the care of the bus conductor. He in turn put me off the bus when I arrived at my school. One morning, there I was downstairs standing in the aisle, all the seats were full. I held the handrail very tightly. A woman sitting close by smiled at me and then it happened, my knickers fell down. They lay at my feet like a dark brown crumpled carrier bag. I was five. In that split second I realised that I didn't know what to do and I wanted my daddy, but he wasn't there and my knickers were, so after what seemed an age, I stepped out of my knickers and very carefully, trying not to fall over as the bus went on its way, I screwed them up and put them in my pocket where they made a big bulge because the pocket was smaller than the knickers.

The lady who had smiled at me looked at me again and beamed. She said "good girl" and suddenly I knew that everything was all right, that it wasn't the end of the world if your knickers fell down round your ankles because here was someone who said "good girl". I knew in that split second that I had done the right thing. Thanks to that wise woman, I didn't feel embarrassed, the happening was just part of life. As I got off the bus, the lady whispered in my ear "don't forget to tell them at school that your elastic's gone." I thanked her and got off the bus thinking my elastic's not gone it's still in my knickers. It was later of course I realised exactly what she had meant. Since that time, my elastic has gone, metaphorically speaking, more times than I can remember! I just keep picking up the knickers or whatever else.

Many people spend a great deal of their time wondering what other people will think. What other people will think of their appearance, their belongings, their jobs, their way of life. It's interesting to note that if you stand in a room full of people gathered together for some social function and you take the trouble to listen carefully, you will find that a great many of the sentences being spoken by people begin with the word "I". If so many sentences begin with "I" how can a great many people be noticing us as individuals. If they are not noticing us then surely they cannot be too bothered about our possessions, belongings, jobs etc. etc. etc. and yet we allow ourselves feelings of embarrassment about what they, these people might think. If Norman Wisdom had stopped to think about embarrassment, he could never have gone on. He took embarrassment, shook it, having first grasped it securely and then made it work for him. He turned it into humour — clever man.

Some years ago I was invited as a guest speaker to a very large gathering in London. A thousand people filled a huge hall and there was I, engaged to speak for the whole of the afternoon, on the podium. I was to keep these people interested and occupied, to stimulate them, but most of all to encourage them to leave at the end of the day feeling much more positive and healthy. A tall bill. As usual I welcomed the challenge.

It was a fairly bright morning as I stood there, I remember the sun shining through the windows. I started to speak and all was well. The same old feeling came over me that always comes as I look at an audience, a feeling of warmth and of wanting to know them better. I must have been speaking for about 20 minutes in all when suddenly my mind went completely blank. It wasn't that I just couldn't remember what I was saying, I couldn't even remember where I was. Never having used notes, I stood opening and closing my mouth like the proverbial fish out of water. No words came, just the opening and closing of the facial aperture. The lady who had asked me to speak hurried to the stage, climbed the little steps at the side and scurried towards me.

"Are you alright?" she said. "No" I said. "Oh dear." She went pale at the thought that I had, like the actress, forgotten my lines. "What will you do?" she asked. I didn't answer. By this time there was an awful lot of fidgeting going on in the audience, clearly visible in the front rows. Then I had what we used to call a "brainwave" (where did that phrase come from? Nevertheless we used to say it, perhaps some people still do). I cleared my throat and hoped that something would come in the shape of words. They came, standing there with the aid of the microphone. I told everyone in the room that I had forgotten where I was up to, had forgotten what I was saying and most of all, forgotten the whole topic of my lecture. I asked them to give me a few minutes to gather my wits in the vain hope that I might remember these things and be able to continue. After I had spoken the worried lady organiser, clasping and unclasping her hands before her said "Oh if only you had used notes" as though the using of notes would have prevented this, as she saw it, near disaster.

47

Then it happened. A lady wearing a lilac coloured suit and almost matching hat, stood up. She was about twelve rows back from the podium, to my right, she stood up and began to clap, not the slow dread clap that entertainers fear but a brisk applause.

Within seconds, another woman was on her feet, then a man near the back, another man to my far left, a woman in the front row, a teenager in the middle of the audience. In no time at all they were all on their feet clapping and smiling. Suddenly I knew where I was. I knew exactly the point I had reached before I dried up. I remembered everything. It was possible to continue but there was something that had to be done immediately.

I thanked them and asked the audience to sit down and then through the microphone I asked the woman in the lilac suit if she would stand up again and this she did. I asked her why she had decided to applaud and before she could answer I motioned to a technician who hastened to her with a hand mike. "Well" she said, "all of us must have wondered at some time what it would be like to forget our words if we were speaking publicly. Many of us do not do this simply because we feel we couldn't. You were honest enough to say that you had forgotten, you didn't try to deceive us or bumble your way through it, you asked us to try to understand. I applauded because I wanted you to know you at least had my support."

When she finished speaking, applause erupted again. All was well. What could have been a very embarrassing situation had turned into something else, the rest of the afternoon was a huge success and a thousand and one of us laughed and joked and cried and listened and felt that the sharing of each other's company was well worthwhile. We were lucky because the lady in the lilac suit cared enough about me as another human being to show that she would support me and she did, and helped to alleviate my embarrassment.

Norman Wisdom's laughter, his constant falling over, his shambling, ambling gait, his askewed cap, his ill-fitting suit, all of him, he gave as a gift to us. Do we laugh at Norman because we feel embarrassed on his behalf? Either way, feeling embarrassed gains nothing at all, it merely proves that we, like the majority of human beings, can make mistakes and also be caught unawares.

How many times have you found yourself walking towards someone. A person that you know. As you get near and they are almost within touching distance you realise that you can't remember their name. It's an awful feeling isn't it? You have known them for years and years, here they are walking towards you and you have forgotten their name. Embarrassing or is it frustrating or indeed a combination of both? What do you do in this simple yet difficult situation? Well you have choices, you can (a) talk to them and not mention any name at all, you could (b) make a guess at their name and get it wrong or (c) you could come out with it and make a joke against yourself. You might well use words like 'you are never going to believe this. You and I have known each other for years, but I must be going off my trolley, I can't for the life of me remember your name!' All too often the other person will laugh. "That happens to me, it happens all the time, isn't it embarrassing, I'm Marjorie." At the sound of the name you are filled with intense relief. Of course it's Marjorie how on earth could you have forgotten. But you did. You couldn't recall the name of the person you had known for ten years.

Afterwards you ask yourself what is wrong, why is it that I forget names. Well again there could be a variety of reasons. We are told that from 30 years of age our brain cells are destroyed quite regularly. Is that a reason? You are busy and anxious, no time for trivia. You are worried about something that has taken precedence over everything else or you're just plain forgetful. It doesn't have to be the major epic of the century, the happening of all time. So you forgot someone's name, believe me if they are mortally wounded by this fact and very upset you have got to ask yourself what sort of a person they are anyway. Ask yourself how you would react if someone told you they had forgotten your name. I can hear you saying "I have to admit I've often found myself in the same position."

Difficulties arise in life, situations that make us feel odd and ill at ease. They need not have this negative effect on us. It's about taking more of life's little difficulties in our stride after all, surely we would be incredibly and most arrogantly boring if we got everything right all of the time.

Don't you struggle to get even a part of it right for part of the time? I do.

There is no death only a
change of worlds

Seattle (Seatlh) (1786-1866)
Suquamish Chief

Bereavement

Someone we love has died. Someone who means a great deal to us can no longer laugh or cry, touch or caress, speak or call. Someone we love is dead and in their place is emptiness and pain. We want them here, returned to us, so that we can be free of all the sentences that start with the words if only.

When death comes it leaves behind so much. If only I hadn't nagged your father, says the houseproud mother. I'd give anything for the mud from his boots to be on the carpet now.

But yesterday, last week, last year, it was a chore and she believed that she would have forever to nag him for he was hers and they had their life together.

The husband, grieving for his wife now dead, wishes that he had shown her more appreciation on long tedious shopping expeditions, and that perhaps he had said I love you more often.

And then there are those of us who lose children. Asking ourselves repeatedly, why, why, why. Why me? Why did God do this to me?

For often in our grieving God bears the brunt of our emotional pain. So many things that go wrong in the world can be blamed on man, but when we speak of death we often see the prime mover to be God.

Now we are left grieving, marooned on an island surrounded by the sea of our own fear, anger, frustration, depression, but seldom joy. And what do we feel if the loved one has died after a terrible illness? Dare we admit our feelings of relief that the pain and the suffering is now over? No longer the wincing with pain, the hospital bed, the stay in the hospice, the constant hurrying and scurrying to give support, all now gone, but dare we say I am relieved? Difficult.

How do we comfort one another? What do we say to those who are bereaved? How do we show them that we care? In our culture we are often very good at sending flowers and cards and these, of course, are so important to the grieving family. Often treasured and kept for years. In many cases never, ever thrown away. But is it enough? Are we giving merely sympathy? I sympathise with you in your sad loss. I understand exactly how you feel. I know what you are going through. And yet in my heart I want to call out to the person who says these words. "No you don't. You don't know exactly how I feel, you don't know what I am going through because he wasn't yours, he was mine". My partner, my father, my brother. She was part of my family, my mother, my sister, my child, and you do not know exactly how I feel, and yet we go on saying the words.

What is sympathy? The dictionary definition of sympathy is state of sharing, or tendency to share emotion, sensation, condition, etc., of another person or thing. So when you sympathise with me do I presume that you are trying to share my emotion, the feelings that I have? I ask myself do you really understand?

Empathy is, however, a different matter. The Greeks tell us that empathy is to stand in the shoes and look out of the eye sockets.

When I am grieving, perhaps I long for you to stand in my shoes and to share with me the feelings of pain, disquiet and utter loss. If you were to give me your empathy then you would in fact, be looking at the world as I see it. I would know then that you understand.

Often difficulties arise in families immediately after the funeral. There is so much to do with death certificates, funerals and flowers, and bills to pay. Usually within the family emerges the leader, not always the natural leader, but a relative who will, in fact, take over and do that which has to be done. Not for this person the hours spent crying and showing visible signs of grief, but only the doing, the energy channelled into every task.

The funeral over, the family look about them to see what should be done next. All too often, a caring daughter or daughter-in-law, will decide that it is time that mum cleared out dad's things. Oh, if I only had one pound for every conversation I have ever had with relatives in which the dialogue is as follows:–

Have you anything of your mother's left? Any article of clothing, something soft to the touch, because your father needs it at the moment.

Often there is nothing left, a whole lifetime cleared away in an afternoon, as busy daughters, sometimes helped by sons, clear out the room. Knicknacks kept which will remind them of a dear mother who is gone, but in the main, clothing dispatched to hospices, Oxfam and charity shops on the high street. But what of the griever? What of the partner who now finds himself sleeping in the arid desert that was once a double bed in their years together, filled with love and passion, now empty?

To whom can this man say I am afraid? Yes, he can

say I miss your mother, I wish she were here, but to whom can he express his deep, deep feeling of loss?

When I am counselling grieving people I suggest to them that they take an article of clothing that has belonged to the dead person, for whom they have felt so much love. I talk to them about the way in which at night they will curl up in a warm bed, and hug the garment to them. Yes I know that they will cry and cry, but perhaps better they cry than they fight to preserve an image of coping, usually designed to help others to cope more ably.

The garment will be hugged and the next day when the bed is made, the duvet cover is thrown back, the garment, be it a nightdress or a summer frock, will fall to the floor, from whence it will be carefully retrieved and folded up and put at the side of the double bed where the warm familiar body has lain for so long.

Time passes, and eventually one morning the grieving partner places the nightdress under the pillow, and then much later still, it falls to the floor and is retrieved and folded carefully and put in the drawer. This is the time of goodbyes for the grieving partner, not the time foisted upon him by well-meaning relatives, he has said his goodbyes at his own speed.

A health visitor telephoned me recently. I was unavailable in the office and my secretary answered. It was a strange message on the pad, it said tell Vera there is a cap on the hallstand. I knew exactly what she meant. She had telephoned me some weeks before to explain that she had done exactly as she had learned on one of our courses, with a patient. The old lady regularly took her husband's cap to bed, since it was all that was left of his belongings.

I spoke to the health visitor afterwards. With joy in her voice she told me how she had arrived at the house and seen the cap on the hallstand. Aye, said the woman, and it will stay there. It is the bit of him that will always be here. The treasured cap had made that long perilous journey from the bed to the hallstand. The worst part of the grieving had been endured. A small part of the ordeal already over.

Music plays a great part when we grieve. So many people have our song, or was it the song your mother sang so long ago whenever she was washing up? Or was it the lullaby your child so loved to listen to, when you put her to bed, and now her little bed is empty? Music may catch us unawares, and years afterwards, we find ourselves weeping copiously for something that was passed and is no longer tangible.

But if after the death we take a tape of the music we shared and go into a warm room and sit comfortably in a chair, all the better if we have a cat or a dog to stroke, a pot of tea, the fire on, we play the music, we weep. We play it again, we weep, we weep naturally, we weep in memory, but we have decided to do this for ourselves, we have put ourselves in charge of our own emotions, and never again will that song catch us unawares in quite the same way.

We have named it and claimed it, and though we may never throw it away, it is ours, the memory remains.

For many children, joy comes
as the result of mining
something unique and
wondrous about themselves
from some inner shaft

Thomas J. Cottle

A Bit Of Magic

Many people worry a great deal about the way in which children may react when told of the death of someone they love. Before we talk about how they may or may not react in such circumstances, we need to consider how we as adults respond when given such news, how we as individuals react. Having thought about our reactions, then and only then should we begin to look at our children and their responses. It is a fact that anxious mums often create anxious small miniature people who on seeing the outward signs of distress become distressed themselves, often without knowing why. These small people need reassurance. If such reassurance is not forthcoming from the parent then the child's own view of the world can be spoiled and limited.

This limitation is not about age or about development, it is about the messages that children receive from the adults nearest to them. Try to imagine the tiny baby in the pram or cradle as a receiver so complex, so clever that it is open to all and any messages. What a chastening thought that is! I cannot help but smile, recalling the gossipy conversations between young mums, overheard by small children/receivers!

When the death of someone we love happens, we often feel a variety of feelings, our emotions run high. It may be that we put off the explanation to children believing that there will be a better time. Is there ever a better time to tell a four year old that his brother is dead? A better time to explain why his daddy won't be there any more? I believe that the better time never

comes and as we wait for it and as we convince ourselves that "children don't understand", we devalue
and lessen the relationship we have with them.

A "gentle giant" of a man once needed to talk to me
about his experiences when his brother died. He and
his younger brother shared a bedroom. When he was
about nine years old, he awakened during a particular
summer's night. He remembered seeing his mother
beside his brother's bed. In his sleepy haze he also
thought that he saw his father in the room, but he was
a small boy tired from a long day spent playing happily
with his brother. He merely turned over and went
back to sleep. When he awakened the next day, he was
surprised to find that not only was his brother
obviously up and about before him but that same
brother had actually remembered to make his bed.

On reaching the kitchen, there was no sign of his
brother. When he enquired as to where his brother
was, his mother looked down at the floor and it was
then he realised that she was crying and that something was very wrong. Noone explained. Before he was
to go to school, neighbours and relatives came into the
familiar warm kitchen and spoke in whispers whilst
he, the then small, worried and anxious person longed
to know what was happening and just where his
brother was. A feeling of great, indescribable fear
overwhelmed him. This fear grew and intensified.

When his father, who was renowned for never
having missed a day's work, walked into the kitchen he
knew that something was very very wrong. It was then
he discovered that he was not to go to school although
he knew it was a school day! This little boy actually
spent the next six days with a neighbour, and kindly

though she was she would not go against the wishes of the family and explain what had happened. The then boy, now the grown man, wept as he recalled those days. The days of waiting and searching for the brother whom he was never to see again. Of the kindly now embarrassed neighbour, overheard saying to her husband, believing her young charge to be out of earshot "it isn't right Tom, he should know, let me tell him". The gruff masculine reply "no it isn't for us to say anything, they must have good reason".

Whatever their reasons, kindly misguided, simple or ignorant, they, the family, the parents, have caused their son years of anguish and pain. This man who was once their own loving little boy has suffered greatly. "Why didn't they tell me?" he asked. "I could have coped with knowing he was dead. I had to when a boy at school told me that he was, but then I went back home and pretended that I didn't know because I thought that they mustn't be able to cope because they hadn't told me. It felt like a secret." He cried with me during the counselling sessions. He cried not only for himself as a man but for the special little grieving boy he was all those years ago. He shed a great many tears.

Children do need to know. Many parents seem to have the motto of closed organisations who give information to the workforce only on a "need to know" basis. Parents who decide that a child doesn't need to know then often complacently carry on with their lives believing they have done the right thing.

A young woman taking part in one of my workshops talked of how she didn't like pictures of country cottages with garden gates. She said she hated them, especially when there were children playing in the garden or standing by the gate. We talked of the work of Victorian artists who often painted children in houses and gardens and produced such works of art. "Horrible" she said, "wouldn't have one in the house". She raised her voice, it was harsh and the other people in the group noted her anger as she struggled to contain it. It was only later that she was able to talk about her real reason for disliking these pictures.

She explained that her grandma whom she loved greatly, became ill. She as a very small child watched the ailing grandma. She at five years of age was able to discern that grandma's strength was failing fast and that she had to spend longer and longer in bed. This little girl also noticed that grandma didn't have rosy cheeks any more. This same little girl noticed that grandma's skin felt different. One day on returning from school, she saw an ambulance outside her house. She knew instinctively that the ambulance had come to take grandma to hospital. Grandma had moved in with them some weeks before because she was ill. She ran into the house to find that she was right, her father explained that grandma had indeed gone to the hospital.

She wept as she told us that everyday she waited at the gate for grandma to return. Grandma never did, the weeks and months passed and you can imagine the agony of this small child waiting for this much loved grandma to return. "Where is grandma?" she would ask. "Coming soon" she would be told. Eventually she ceased to ask anymore and when in later life she asked her mother and father why they had never told her the truth, her mother replied "oh you wouldn't have understood darling, you were far too young. We did the right thing, in the end you forgot", but of course she didn't forget. That child, that little girl, now a woman, has never ever forgotten.

Children very often have a clearer perception of symbols than we adults. I find that by using symbols, children are helped to understand, even the youngest child can endeavour to see more clearly what a situation is about. In these days of hi-fi, super duper computers, technology beyond belief, it can be easy to lose sight of a child's need for simple symbols or simple magic, and yet, through all of our progress, through all of the developments and achievements within the world, from space walking to "see whose calling" phones, the tooth fairy not only persists but has now created an industry of her own.

There are special pouches and cushions in which to place the precious tooth. For almost all adults over the age of twenty-five, the tooth fairy has been a part of life. Out dropped that first milk tooth, to be placed lovingly either under the pillow or in some other secret place — ah! the effort of parents trying to prevent the child from making the place too secret without betraying the identity of the tooth fairy. "Well darling, perhaps the tooth fairy isn't used to finding little teeth inside the back of the wardrobe." The tooth fairy was and is extremely important. For many present day children she is part of the symbolism of childhood, come to think of it, she may have been a part of the symbolism of your childhood.

A man, very grumpy, once said "rubbish Mrs. Waters, I never believed in the tooth fairy". "How sad" I said, "it shows!" He grumped his way out of my company.

Having established that belief in this fairy lives on, what about the belief in small time magic? Don't we all need a bit of magic in our lives? Of course we do. We can wrap death in a little magic if we try hard enough. The mum who says "grandpa has gone to Jesus" uses the magic of religion, hoping that the child will believe that grandpa is safe, though unseen, with the friendly Jesus, still to be looked after and made safe. It is a fact that young children believe in magic if they are introduced to it at an early age.

When I want to explain to a child about death I talk about parcels and packages. I explain that our bodies are a kind of package, a kind of parcel. A very important wrapping for a very important something. Everyone of us is precious, more precious than words can ever say. The most precious part of us is inside where noone can see. It is shiny and sparkles and never dies and because it is so very precious, because it is such a treasure, we need something to keep it in so we keep it in a package. That package is called a body. Our bodies keep the shiny, precious bit safe. Sometimes packages get damaged or torn, sometimes ripped and destroyed. Eventually, the package has to go. When this happens we die but no matter what, nothing at all can destroy the precious, shiny part of us that is inside. When someone dies, the package is no use any more, it is finished. The shiny part will never be finished, it lives on and although we are not clever enough to see the shiny, precious part, this part of us rises up and soars into the sky. If you want to see where the precious part has gone, you need to look into the night sky. As you look into that sky you will see lots of shiny stars. They are really the precious parts of people. Those who don't know about this magic say they are just stars but we know that they are a shining precious part of those we love who have died.

Children cope better with knowing, especially if the knowing holds a magic explanation and if the voice that explains is full of love.

A woman in her late twenties rang me recently to tell me that she still watched the stars at night. I did not recognise her voice, she reminded me of my words and my little story that she had first heard eighteen years ago after her father died. She rang because she simply wanted me to know that she had been greatly helped by this explanation and although as an adult she had realised it couldn't possibly be true, she still felt as she looked at the stars that there was something special about them.

If you doubt that this story would actually help a child in such a situation then it would only be fair to say that there are exceptions to all rules but until you have held the warm hand of a small child and looked with him into the night sky, until you have watched the tears roll down his face as he says "goodnight daddy", until you have these experiences, you have no proof that magic doesn't work.

It is as natural to die

as to be born.

Francis Bacon

Additional pieces on bereavement are included in Vera Waters' first book, *Half a Rainbow*.

May you live all
the days
of your life

Jonathan Swift

On Being Jilted

Jilted. A good old fashioned word jilted, it apparently comes from way back in history. One dictionary definition says "to cast off (a lover) after encouraging." Well, that certainly is an apt description of what jilting is all about.

Some people live alone, never linking up to another to create a larger unit. Often they admit that they feel happiest in their own company. By being able to cope with yourself, without another, is for many an exercise in self discipline. However we can so easily be cast into the Alone state quite abruptly with cries of 'oh I never knew!'

Our society in its very patterns still leads the young and up and coming teenager to believe that coupling is not only the norm but a necessity. One thing is certain. If you have spent a period of your life wrapped in the love of another human being, if you have shared home and possessions then to lose that person suddenly can fill you with total and utter grief. The whole experience turns us from a logical adult into a crying child. Still the propaganda continues and, as ever, the young person in our society believes that falling in love is an essential part of life's rich pattern.

If death were the thief that robbed us of the one we loved then we can woefully and acceptingly mourn. Other people can see our grieving. They send gestures of thoughtfulness and empathy, flowers and cards arrive and provide for us small crumbs of comfort at this most difficult of times. On being jilted there are often no cards or flowers or gestures of goodwill.

We can usually depend on the fact however that there will be much gossip and speculation, often by those who have carried the banner, the flag of friendship above their heads.

On being jilted we are left with a sense of failure. If not at the very beginning of the process, the sense of failure will come during or even after. Does time heal, it's an old adage that suggests that it does. It is my belief that time doesn't necessarily heal. What does happen is that because life has to go on we force ourselves into the next twenty four hour capsule and work through it, and in so doing use up the energy that we would need to mourn more deeply in this Alone State.

Often it is the lot of the jilted person to remain in a house full of memories. If you are that person you will find yourself sitting in the same familiar room looking at the furniture and everything that has gone to make a house into your home. Looking around you, you see a picture that you bought together. You hear again, in your mind, your shared laughter and separately the laughter of your partner. The hugs, the kisses, the joy of that day seem to surround you. From the picture you look to the rest of the room, the carpet, ah yes, the pattern that he didn't like but you did. You coerced and cajoled and insisted and here you are left with that same carpet. Upstairs the slippers still beside the bed as though waiting to remind you that your lover will not return. You know that he or she has gone never to return, usually belonging now however briefly to another, possibly with a younger person full of life and vitality whilst you, the jilted one grow older by the second.

The jilter on the other hand has places to go and people to see, clothes to buy for the new image. Not the man or woman you love but a stranger. A person who looks different yet has the same mannerisms and a familiar voice. You still love and want your partner who now speaks of other people as though he or she is a stranger and you should understand.

Nobody tells us how to cope with the pain of rejection. The anxiety that accompanies this feeling is immeasurable, the knowing that the person you love is now with another person whom they now love. All that you are left with is the emptiness and the void.

It is at these times that it seems that every song ever written seems to be about love lost, love found, love missed, love dying or love eternal. The lyrics do nothing to help support or uplift you. It is a good idea at this time to make sure you have all non vocal tapes in the car as you can be driving along and suddenly find yourself becoming tearful as a singer puts into words the very thoughts that are in your head and in your mind.

And then again there is that familiar home. In its way it can be comforting but in another way is not comforting at all, for every time you sit in that same room where you both sat together for so long your world seems full of memories. Why not break the pattern — go out and buy a new lamp, a nest of coffee tables, an ornament, a new rug, something that will stop the pattern passage of your thoughts. Yes you will still look at the picture, you will still remember the carpet and then your eyes will fall on the nest of coffee tables that you bought yourself after the parting, then you will be forced to remember that you went into a shop, on your own, and chose the tables carefully and took them home. There are no thoughts of your lover connected with those tables, only thoughts of the new you striving to survive.

If there are some particular items in your home that cause you to become emotional at the most unexpected times then put them away for a while. A great many people take down all the photographs, put them in drawers. A sense of temporary healing often accompanies this action but the tearing up of photographs should be considered carefully, especially wedding photographs because as you cut across the smiling images of the couple encaptured within the frame remember that you cut across yourself. It is a great shame to cancel out all the love that there has been. In that lovely song from "Chess" sung by Elaine Page and Barbara Dickson there is a line that says "No one is completely on your side. Would we love them if they were?"

As in most other kinds of grieving process caused by whatever reason, the double bed when occupied by one person becomes an arid desert of loneliness. Where once when going early to bed we had luxuriated in the fact that we could stretch our legs and arms to the four points of the double or king size bed now we want only to touch the person who shared it with us, but they are there no longer.

It is a fact that after being jilted many people experience great difficulty in going to sleep. Take a pillow and lay it where your partner would have been, you will find that during the night your arm will go round the pillow and you will comfort yourself, making the bed seem less empty than it really is. As the days go by and form themselves into weeks try new recipes, make meals that you have not shared with the person who has now gone, try new ideas. If you can afford it, or do it yourself, change the decoration in the lounge or bedroom, make something in your home different so that you too can grow with that change and having done this then look in your wardrobe and ask yourself is it time for you to look different, is it time for you to look at having a new image even though there is no one new in your life, no princess for the glass slipper, no prince charming to steal you away.

It is worth remembering at such times that in order for another door to open we have to have doors that close in our life. It sounds like a cliché to say that as one door opens another one closes but isn't that exactly what happens in so many instances? If, at this moment you have been recently rejected, you will not believe as you read these words that you will have a new life. Yet look around, there are people whom you know have had this experience and who are now happily in relationships with other people. The greatest difficulty with being jilted is the fact that it saps the confidence so badly that it makes us feel as though we are not only unworthy but unlovable. We start to grow when we realise that no relationship is really one hundred percent safe and that if our partner leaves us, albeit for another, we have to eventually get to the point where we accept that if the relationship had been a hundred percent then our partner would not be with someone else. It is easy to neglect a relationship, to get it wrong, to forget that dotting the i's, crossing the t's is an important part of making a lasting relationship. The thoughtfulness, the kindness and the support, remain long after the loving lust is gone.

When you have cried for what seems like forever, when you have hidden away and not dared to go out, when you have drunk yourself silly, when you have eaten yourself sick, when you have starved yourself and lost weight, when you have done any or all of these things then it is time to start anew. Painstakingly and carefully compile a list of your likes and dislikes, these are your preferences, they are about you as a single person and not as part of a pair. Even the most simple questions at this time in your life are capable of making you feel incredibly sad. Write the answers anyway and when you have finished read through your list. Preface what you read with the words "I am a person who likes the colour red, enjoys music by the Beatles, goes fishing, jogging, likes to read about golf, hates very hot weather" and so on and so forth.

You might easily feel at this point that nothing would be gained by doing this but the discipline that will keep you in one piece, in one functioning piece, has to start somewhere. It starts in small ways when we take part of ourselves to ourselves and exert some control. Before you can cope fully with the knowledge that you have been jilted you need to know who the person was, who fits into that category, you are well aware that you know the person who went off and did the dirty deed, but you need to know what kind of a person he or she left behind. Oh, and by the way, it isn't a good idea to step right into the market place, to do yourself up like a dog's dinner and to go out and actively look for another partner. Remember the logic in your personality is found within the adult part of

71

your thinking. When we are bereaved, sad, jilted, anxious and don't know where to turn, it is the child in us that functions at the highest level. Our child has little or no logic. If we go into the market place too early then we will find ourselves in a bigger mess then ever, with someone we don't really like who just momentarily showed us a little kindness and consideration. To go too early into the market place is to take with us an invisible begging bowl. We carry it before us saying mutely "I am hurt, rejected and confused, please love me." Some people, although still carrying the bowl and giving the same message, decide to put on a brave outward face and go into a pattern of going out with other people merely to get even with the opposite gender.

Our society doesn't help when it comes to getting on with life without a partner. Suddenly a woman who has had many friends safe within relationships of their own finds herself without so many friends. Overnight she has become the 'femme fatale,' she doesn't feel any differently but certain of her friends view her now as a single woman obviously on the look out for another man. Men are often wooed by dinner party hosts, neighbours, people who have friends who are single, in other words the matchmaking begins. Often the rejected man does not want to be part of this scene at all and as for the femme fatale, well curled up at home in an empty overlarge double bed, she wonders how mistaken everyone can be.

If you have never been to the cinema or sat in a restaurant on your own, paid a bill, signed a cheque or simply taken responsibility for what goes on in the administrative side of your home, then losing your partner can cause tremendous upheaval and problems. Without the respectability of the widow's weeds help can be very slow at coming! It is at this time that many people wish they had learned to be more independent, to do more, to be more confident as in the case of a woman fitting a plug. To be able as a man to choose your own clothes and to know that they look right. The Alone State zaps our emotional confidence, suggesting to us that we can't cope. Remember that you can. It is a good idea to stay out of the limelight, even to steel yourself into the self discipline that keeps you away from friends just for a short while. Remember that whilst you are talking in detail to a so called friend about the ins and outs of your broken relationship, you may well be telling more than one person. The lives of others can become very very interesting even if in fact the listener's life has very little in it that one could call scintillating. The estranged couple become like a pair of actors on a stage, their friends often an over participatory audience who give not only advice but firm controlling suggestions.

Try taking small steps, one at a time. The goal for one week could be actually doing something on your own that you haven't done before; for a second week it could be about changing something in the house, and for the third week changing something about your appearance. Set your goals, work to them, try not to be too downhearted if you don't reach them.

A lovely man who was once in this position described himself as feeling as though he were a small boy learning about things he should have known long ago. Having become exasperated with the inner workings of the washing machine he decided to go out and use the launderette. One visit to the launderette and he was back trying to find the booklet that told him what to do with the machine. "I have never been mechanically minded" he said, "left everything to do with household appliances to her, felt it was her job, wife, mother all of that you know but after sitting in that launderette with an inquisitorial female I felt more vulnerable than I have ever felt in my life, and the only person I wanted was my wife."

Coping with being jilted isn't easy, it never was and it never will be and it takes time to get confidence back, to look in the mirror and like the person that you see there. Remember small steps, one at a time, and as I have said earlier in this section, remember that at times of crises you need to live in twenty four hour capsules, consider yourself a successful winner as you survive one day, passing to the next, keep moving! That's the secret, keep surviving!

Try to avoid encouraging your friends, relatives and acquaintances to talk freely with you about your private life. Parts of our lives are private, yet when we are rejected or jilted these parts often become public as though everyone we know has a right to know the most gory details. Remember that with relationships people have very varied codes of pattern of behaviour. Every time we talk about the other man or the other woman we introduce them into the room in which we sit, we bring them in. They do not need to be tangibly present, they are there in our speech and in our thoughts. We are introducing them to friends who say "what's she like?" "what is he like?" "is she younger?" and so it goes on. Unless it was your idea and your ambition as a child to be an actor or actress then look at the situation carefully and you will find that that is fast what you are becoming.

Friends will allow you to be the visiting cabaret, only for as long as it suits them and then they are faced with the inevitable question of whether or not to be friendly, to continue the friendship with the jilter and the jilted. You may feel very much betrayed when a dear friend tells you that she or he is going to keep in contact with the partner who has deserted you. Not everyone can be loyal to one party. It is evident not only in the political field but in our private lives. Other people cannot cancel out the days, the weeks, the outings, the experiences they have shared with you as a couple, taking sides is very very difficult. Your partner may well have jilted you but ask yourself why. Did you do enough, did you keep the relationship young and vibrant in itself or did you neglect it, take it for granted and cease to work at it?

Because we are so dependent one upon the other we are devastated when the person we love leaves us. It is at this time once again we must try to learn to love ourselves a little more.

In many ways grieving for someone who is dead brings with it respectability. Grieving for someone who simply gets up and walks out of our lives leaves no such respectability. Instead of sympathy we are often met with criticism and cries of "I told you so." There are no flowers to cheer us and no cards to put upon the mantelpiece, to prove that other people sympathise with our sad loss. Often the garment of mourning is denied us and only those who are our true friends will continue to give us support.

However being jilted need not be the end of our life. Although during the experience we often wish that it could be so. The grieving process begins and as in all mourning experiences changes start to take place. If you make a decision to try to rebuild your life then you have taken the very first step on the positive road to recovery. You will never forget the experience, it cannot be totally forgotten, not only because of its pain content but also because it is such a difficult learning experience.

Take it as part of your life!

Name it!

Claim it!

Then throw it away!

Who knows at some time in the future when you meet a person who really cares about you, you may feel like sending a thank you card to the person who originally jilted you.

Life passes
Like a drift of silk chiffon
Slipping
Thro' the fingers of time

Vera Waters

Never bear more than one kind
of trouble at a time. Some
people bear three — all they
have had, all they have now,
and all they expect to have.

Edward Everell Hale (1822–1909)
American writer and clergyman

Imagine a clock

Imagine a clock. A clock that tells us that the time is 12 o'clock, 12 o'clock noon or 12 midnight. It is not the hour that we should think about but the position of the hands both together joined on the figure 12.

Imagine that you are standing in life at 12 o'clock precisely. That you are standing just like the hands of the clock pointing from the centre to the number 12. You are upright. Standing in the present. If you turn the clock back to 11.45 you will be firmly in the past, 15 whole minutes into the past. If you turn the clock to 12.15 you will be firmly in the future. To take this example further try now to imagine that as you stand at 12 o'clock you are standing in a very worthwhile place, a good place to be, the present. All we can really be sure of is the present, the exact moment in which we stand. Looking back in our life transports us into the past and yet there is nothing there that can be changed. Nothing whatsoever can be changed even in the smallest way because it has already happened and therefore is unalterable.

All those words and actions which we know we have said and done we cannot take back, nor can we pretend that they have never ever happened. We cannot erase them or change them in any way. They have already been stated, uttered, proclaimed and heard by others. Yet not everything in the past is negative, much is positive and that is why our golden days, those days which contain the happy memories, can be stored and used to help us through.

Usually when we are tired and thoughtful, feeling

low or anxious, recalling the past rarely conjures up positive pictures, instead we usually remember everything we did wrong. If however we briefly consider what we perceive to be our mistakes and make a decision to try not to repeat them in the future, then our awareness is heightened and our personal growth progresses and what is more we will give ourselves more peace of mind. It is at this juncture that we can make a resolution and as we stand on the clock face of life at 12 o'clock we can decide that in the future we will not say the words we have said in the past.

What will bring about change? We cannot be sure that when the future comes we will not make similar comments or actions. But we can be sure about the minute in which we stand.

A great many problems in life are caused by the fact that as human beings many of us worry about our past experiences. It is a myth to believe that if we think about these experiences and consider them deeply then we will in some way bring about some healing.

Many have had the experience of an unhappy childhood, spent with unhelpful or uncaring people, or merely parents whose level of ignorance was high and whose level of sensitivity was low, such people will have experienced a past where love has been very very scarce but thinking about that childhood is not going to change what has happened. Standing at 12 o'clock firmly in the present you can make a decision to bring about actual change in your own life. You could even decide how you will speak to someone else, how you will behave, what you will do, where you will go. You can make a decision to be more considerate, more courteous, more well mannered or you can make a decision to be irritable, abrasive and abrupt.

Standing at 12 o'clock you can make these decisions and put them into practice.

Imagine now the hands of the clock telling us that the time is 12.15. There are many people who worry about the future. They actively dwell on it. Once I saw a cartoon of a man in a bowler hat, hunched shoulders, rubbing his hands together, a mournful expression on his face. Underneath the caption read "I am eagerly awaiting my next disappointment." Imagine ruining the prospects of the future by always expecting the worse.

"What will I do if I don't get the job, what will I do if the house doesn't sell, what will I do if he says he doesn't love me?" Winston Churchill once said "too many ifs accumulate". Elsewhere in this book I mention the way in which when someone dies so many of our sentences start with the words if. If only I hadn't shouted at him, if only I'd been more considerate, if only I had let her have that new dress, if only, if only. Those ifs belong in the past, nothing can be changed.

The ifs we place in the future give us cause for a great deal of worry however, because if we spend our time worrying constantly about the past and the future, there is very little that can be achieved as we stand on the clock face of life at 12 o'clock.

This is the present. This is the time to make change. If you feel the need to be different then make it now. If you want to improve the quality of your life or the life of someone else then do it now. Wishful thinking as we sit in a comfortable chair on a winter's evening talking about how we are going to live our life in the spring is all very well but we may not be around when spring-time comes. We need to be doing something now. This is the present.

Nothing is worth more
than this day

Johann Wolfgang von Goethe (1749-1832)

It is interesting to listen to the conversations of others, for conversations show us many, many aspects of someone's personality. A great deal of my time now is spent training professionals. Usually when the training is under way I watch their faces change. They start to look anxious and then eventually some brave soul will say "why didn't I know about this years ago, I've made so many mistakes."

It would be so easy at that time for me or any other trainer to say "you should have known better" but it would be entirely pointless. What I do suggest is that nothing can be done about the past, it cannot be changed but we could start now bringing about change. Recently a police officer looked aghast when in the course of training he learned of the way in which the news of death affected people. "I could have done my job a great deal better" he said, "I should have done it better, I should have known. What I am learning here is common sense, why didn't I know it". On many occasions we miss the complex message wrapped in a simple action and on other occasions we seek to complicate that which would be better understood when simplified. Always I explain to people who reach this point that although nothing can be done about the past they can never, ever, with a free conscience and a good

81

heart make those same mistakes again because this time they know the difference. Being aware and knowing the difference is what enhances our life.

12 o'clock and all's well.

12 o'clock and here I stand straight to the point, firmly in the middle of my own present.

Recently in the course of a workshop one of those present was talking to me about my work. He described some aspects of how he saw my behaviour and then he said you are just like a coiled string. Of course, following on from his other comments I immediately thought he had said a coiled spring. When realisation dawned we laughed together. In fact I went on laughing for quite some time for in my mind there came a picture. First of all, a box containing a tightly coiled spring which when opened boinged and boinged about, springing out of the box onto a surface and going along its way and then I thought of a coiled string. I imagined myself looking into the box and seeing this worn old piece of string carefully placed in a few circles inside the box. Not going boing and not capable of going anywhere. Now if I had wanted to take a negative approach I could have been offended but I wasn't. I saw the laughter and the kindness in his face and I knew that there was not even the smallest chance that he meant anything but humour and fun by his comment.

At a conference once I listened to a very pompous man speak for boring hour after boring hour on a platform. As the audience were given permission to go and seek the solace of the cup that cheers in the interval I overheard one smartly garbed businessman say to another "that man is a legend in his own lunchbox". I found the comment hilarious having listened to the pomposity of this boring speech for hours, and the thought of him cramped and crumpled inside a lunchbox gave me a feeling of warmth that seemed to come up from my toes.

Humour is often linked very closely with confidence or indeed lack of it. So many of our comedians have stood on the edge of a nervous breakdown and looked inside a trough of despond. It takes confidence or the illusion of confidence to share our humour with others. Humour like laughter embraces others, takes them in, enfolds them and gives them permission to smile. Have you ever walked along the street smiling at people. The last time I did it one woman said to another "do you know her," "no" said the second woman, "neither do I" said the first, "silly beggar." But it was worth it to watch their faces, so I went back down the street and said "hello ladies, lovely day isn't it, no you don't know me, God's in his heaven and all's well with the world". They scurried off, giggling and laughing, it was worth it, it gave them something to smile about although I suppose it could be counted as very eccentric behaviour on my part! — and when it happened it happened in the present — the 'now' standing at 12 o'clock.

Yesterday is but
A reflection
Today is now
Tomorrow is a bonus

Jim Billingsley

83

Happiness is in the
comfortable companionship
of friends

Pam Brown, 1928

Friendship

Friendship is love. Friendship enriches our lives and makes life's passage easier. The love of a friend is invaluable. True friendship cannot be bought, coerced or diminished. Good friends function out of a loving union, links in a chain, friend to friend, trust to trust. Patience to patience, tolerance to even more tolerance and so the friendship grows.

A good friend is one who you call in the night saying "please come, please come," "I am on my way" replies the friend. No enquiry, no questions — "what do you want? what is the matter?" simply "I am coming to be with you whatever the problem."

A true friend, woman to woman, notices the bags under your eyes, the dark patches almost hidden by clever makeup. A true friend man to man notices that you are less tolerant, that you are smoking and drinking more than usual. A true friend knows when there is a tiredness in your voice and a very good and close friend telephones you just as you are about to make the call yourself.

A friend knows the colours you prefer, the food you like to eat, your pet hates and fears, whilst the truest of all friends bathes in your reflected glory as you receive recognition for an action or work well done. This is indeed true friendship without envy, jealousy or petulance, a relationship based on love. What kind of a friend are you?

God gave us our relatives;
Thank God we can choose
our friends

Ethel Watts Mumford

In life most of us need positive friendships, however friendships that become weighty sometimes become extremely strained. Very recently I strained a friendship considerably. Things were happening in my life that were hurting me a great deal. I became blind to the needs of a very dear friend. His needs were not my concern, because in my need of him I wanted his response and his support, so that he could help me. I was moaning and bewailing a situation which, in fact, I could not change and during this period I missed his birthday. I had never, ever, missed his birthday, and I have known him for 20 years, but this year I did. You see I didn't really share, I was too busy taking from the friendship.

When working I found that I was able to switch off that negative part of my personality, but when I met with this good and trusted friend, when he hugged me and helped me, I loaded him up with the weight of my problems.

Eventually, he grew tired of saying "it can't be changed, you are losing your peace of mind." Then I became angry with him, because I felt that there should be more to the situation than there was. I wanted him to offer solutions which he could not do. And so we came to a situation in which he grew tired of my constant taking, so much so that for a brief time he absented himself from my life. It was only then, when he was no longer there to call upon, that I looked in on my own selfishness. It's so easy to say to friends they should be able to give or take whatever we need, but even friendship has its limitations because it requires us to 'work at it' just like any other relationship. It is about give and take, and sadly, in this situation, all I was doing was taking.

What are your friendships like? When did you last look at them? When did you last measure how much you give and how much take? A week, a month, a year, is it so long since you evaluated what friendship is really about? It's so easy to become someone who is seen to be a very sound and stable individual, but who privately needs a great deal of support and help. We can lean on our friends but that leaning can become so burdensome to the trusted friend, that eventually, they, in their weariness, creep away, or even worse, start to avoid us in subtle ways that we cannot quite measure. The friend may stoically continue to give support until one day, bursting at the seams, they say "for goodness sake, when did you last think of me?" Then we are brought rapidly to a halt, and in the mirror, should we care to look, we would see the reflection of our own selfishness.

Friendship is about trusting and it is true, as George Eliot said, that we should not have a need to weigh words but friendship is about the balance between giving and taking. It matters so much that an imbalance does not readily occur. Sometimes a group of people working together in a shop, an office, a bank, a hospital, may get on very well. Daily they exchange chat and gossip. Some of them have particular friendships within the group. Within that group is someone who talks so much about his or her problems, that the group eventually becomes tired and the topic of conversation between the other members is about how they cannot cope with the 'taking' of the one other person. How sad, I wonder if any member of that group is kind enough, and understanding enough, to talk to that person about what he or she is doing. How can we learn if we do not have guidance?

How about stopping now and thinking about your friends. Now is the time to invite that special friend round for a meal. What about that friend who lives quite a way from you, who was so good when you needed them two years ago? When did you last speak on the phone, when did you last send a letter? It is too late when our friends are no longer there to share with. Remember that the other person in the equation could have as many misgivings as you yourself. That person could need your reassurance.

A good way to ease the burden of your lack of confidence is to try to imagine that other people can feel exactly as underconfident as you. Friendship is born out of need. A need for support, help and comfort. Friendships are often formed between people with similar likes, dislikes and interests. It is a way of expressing our needs whilst at the same time we meet the needs of others.

However in order to love others and to attract the love of others into ourselves we first need to value the person we really are. To measure our own talents and gifts! Although we may presume we have little or nothing to offer in terms of friendship there will be something within our personality that can become attractive to others.

When something happens in your life that leaves

you feeling very unhappy it often helps to talk it through with a trusted friend. The sharing of the burden usually causes the sympathetic reaction you need at that time. The sharing helps you to feel comforted. However, as time passes the unhappy experience needs to move from your present into your recent past and hopefully after the passage of further time into the far past. All these stages take time. Often returning to the original friend who still constantly refers to the experience will only serve to keep you in a negative frame of mind. Hindering you when you have decided to feel much more positive.

How often have you felt indebted to a friend who has listened? A person who when you were low gave you support. Remembering that, that same friend cannot necessarily be blamed when he or she refers back to the shared confidence. When we confide our innermost secrets to our friends we actually bear not only our souls but we open our wounds. Avoiding the friend often does not work, only leading to a situation in which there is mistrust and great misunderstanding. Both parties then feel uneasy and unsure of the original friendship.

Why not give your friendship some guidelines? Carefully explain that you found their help at the time of the crisis absolutely invaluable, that you need their help to continue but in a different way because without them you would find it difficult to put the past behind you and get on with your life. A good friend will be understanding and do as you ask.

When you know that you are feeling negative remember that at that time there will be constant withdrawals from your emotional bank. This is not the time to go to see the relative who always has something to moan about. Make the decision to steer clear of those people who will make you feel negative and miserable. Just because at some time they may have listened to you moaning and groaning about life, doesn't give them the right to expect you to do the same at the drop of a hat.

The next time you decide to talk to a friend or relative about your innermost secrets try to remember that the timing of these disclosures can matter a great deal. Before dropping all of your pain on the shoulders of another person try to remember to look at their eyes. Ask yourself "can they take this?" Already by that very thought process, by thinking about another person you are beginning to think positive rather than negative. Because you put the feelings of another person before yourself you help the process to continue.

Surely in this day and age with the celebration of Father's and Mother's Days to say nothing of non smoking days etc, I am sure that someone should have thought of inventing a Friend's Day. If they have, I have not heard of it. However, instead of it being a commercial venture, it should be personal. Tomorrow needs to be the day that you make into a Friend's Day for you! We need our friends, we need our relatives, but often our friends get closer to us than those to whom we are related.

Trusting a friend
is like opening a box and
liking what you find inside

Vera Waters

90

*Do not expect strangers
to do for you what
you can do for yourself*

Quintus Ennius

On Being Sad

Whatever may be written or otherwise stated about the Seasonal Affective Disorder otherwise known as the sad syndrome, it has to be admitted even by the most ardent sceptic that it is usually easier for a person to feel positive in a constructive way on a bright fine day. Darkness for so many of us is synonymous with fear and foreboding. The most successful of horror films are rarely based in total and full light. The most scaring scenes that keep us gripping the arms of our cinema seats need darkness to increase our sense of anxiety and foreboding.

On a bright airy day when the sun shines and we feel neither uncomfortably cold or uncomfortably hot it must be easier to feel just that little bit brighter. All right, all right, I can almost hear some of you telling me that when you feel low the weather, light, bright or dark makes no difference whatsoever. Think again. Take an ordinary day in your life. You live alone. You haven't slept very well the night before but you are not clear as to exactly why this should have been the case. Now it's morning, heavy headed you open the curtains or blinds. The day is dark, dismal and overcast. Just like you. However if when you open the blinds the sun is shining or there is a rainbow in the sky these two facts or happenings can have a good effect on you. Better the day, better the deed!

No, sunshine is not a panacea for all ills. However in many cases light, sunshine and brightness actually help in keeping us feeling much more content with ourselves.

When the autumn and winter evenings begin, create your own little suns. Small lamps strategically placed on tables and shelves create their own pools of individual light. Gently bathing all in that small circle of light, objects are embraced in a warm glow. Look around your home, market stalls, gift shops and thrift shops for the small colourful articles that will give comfort and reflect light in your home. For example, a few coloured glass pebbles placed together on a table beneath a light will trap the reflected light and store it. A brightly coloured dish containing colourful pot pourri will not only brighten the room but fill it with a comforting, welcoming scent. A small doll or tiny teddy again placed beside the lamp will help you to smile as you question its presence there. Conkers, acorns, cones, grouped together in small inexpensive baskets remind us of the earth from which we draw our food and drink.

Treat yourself to fresh flowers each week, these need not be expensive but they make their presence felt within your home. Find a small box or tin and in it place an even smaller mirror. These can be purchased from do it yourself stores as tiny mirror tiles are sold in sheets. Careful placing of a small mirror-tile means that you are able to complete your very special box. Keep the box closed. In the days that follow you will often pick up the box and open it and as you look inside you will either frown or smile as you see your own face reflected there. Centuries ago in the East these boxes were used as part of a healing system. They were known as smiling or laughing boxes.

Another way to help cope with this time of the year is to actually buy yourself a teddy bear. Teddies have been popular for centuries, and a teddy purchased by you knowing it is for you and not for a child can often leave us with varied emotions. A bank manager once said to me that he had walked into a shop and whilst purchasing his teddy had told the shop assistant an amazing tale about a nephew whom he hadn't seen for a long time. The teddy, he had told her, was to be a present for the nephew. Of course this was not the case but he said he felt that he had to let her know that it couldn't possibly be for anyone but a child. Could it be that we have really achieved something in life when we can say, yes, I am buying this teddy for myself, I like it and I am not saying otherwise as a consequence of being bothered by what the shop assistant or anyone else thinks.

Well, having brought your teddy, sit him on the top of the pillow in your bedroom. If your bed is shared by someone else hopefully they will be able to cope with the presence of the teddy. If they can't ask yourself what you are doing in the bed with them! For, if you can't laugh about the teddy together it may be that there is not enough in your relationship that is worth laughing about. On your dark days when you walk into the bedroom you will see the teddy sitting there. On very dark days you may pick him up and hold him and as one lady said "I picked up my teddy and I cried and cried". She then continued 'I felt much better and then I made a cup of tea.'

Today I sent some flowers to someone who does a great deal of work for me, and without whose help and expertise I could not achieve the standard of work which I regard as necessary. He has been in hospital lately and yet, despite convalescing with his own pain and suffering, is always there ready with his advice and eager to make sure that my affairs are in order. I asked the florist to put on the card "Just a bit of cherishing!" Isn't that what we all need, just a bit of cherishing? Well, if there isn't someone in your life to cherish you, especially through the dark and dismal winter periods then start cherishing yourself, knowing that if there is no one else and you are the only person that's left, why not look after yourself, love yourself just a little?

It isn't possible to change the seasons, but it is possible to consider that having a holiday during the autumn or winter months may well help you. That taking time out during these months could prove to be beneficial. That by accepting that during the autumn and winter months you may well need more sleep, you are acknowledging the basic needs not only of your body but very probably your mind.

When we sing everybody hears us
When we sigh nobody hears us.

Russian proverb

Comfort

It seemed an age as we waited on the station. "We need to put the other carriages on" a railway official said. He was resplendent in his uniform suggesting that he knew just what was what. We waited, possibly some 20 people grouped together, some people solitary and alone.

A man came on to the platform with a young boy. A man in his forties, jean-clad, with very shiny shoes clapping his gloved hands together reminding us all that it really was quite cold. The boy surprisingly took off his gloves and rummaged in the inside pocket of his thick, brightly coloured, state of the art coat. Producing a long red tube he unscrewed the top to which was attached a brush coated in a red liquid. Then he proceeded to write on one of the pillars on the platform. His father encouraged him, helping him suggest what words he should use to deface the surface whilst the railway official appeared to look the other way.

Then on to the platform came a small girl, bright eyed beneath a red bob hat. She tightly held her mother's hand as they walked down the platform steps. It was as though only she knew how to smile. She smiled at us all, giving the impression that this was a very exciting day, that travelling on a train should fill us all with joy. I for one forgot the awful parent and his destructive son and became absorbed in the little girl with the smiling face and the rosy cheeks. The young boy stopped his disfiguration of the pillar and looked at her then abruptly put his brush away. The little girl chatted to her mummy. Question after question.

"Is Uncle Frank coming?"

"When is Uncle Frank coming?"

"Will Uncle Frank get here before we have to go?"

At that point a man appeared at the top of the steps leading onto the platform. He waved, catching the child's attention. "Mummy, mummy" she cried.

Mummy looked towards the man, smiled, responded to his waving hand and ran towards him, skirting a group of people chatting together. At that point a small clear voice could be heard saying "mummy, mummy, be careful don't go too near the edge, you might fall and hurt yourself." Mummy looked back at her little girl and the line of love between them was like a comforting ribbon of indestructible strength. The little girl's name was Kate. Kate full of life, full of love, Kate who wanted to make sure that her mummy was safe.

That little girl on that particular day was for me living proof that in this world where we could well be persuaded that nothing but badness ever happens, there is a great deal of goodness. Goodness and love still prevail and always prove to be the strongest, most comforting part of our lives. Without love it is difficult to achieve the fullness of life. Loving in itself does not necessarily have to be from one single person or even a family. It can come from anywhere at anytime as in the case of Kate. Filling the platform with her love. Of course not everyone in that station on that day was aware of Kate's love but for those of us who were, who saw and experienced her personality there was love and in that love comfort could be found.

If we need to be comforted then we must seek out the comforters and in our search appreciate that we too have the capacity to comfort others. The actions of people of any age, creed, colour or description can and will give comfort. A smile, a friendly gesture, a little bit of help can provide comfort to a lonely person who feels that no one really cares.

Recently I met a woman sitting in a wheelchair in front of a large store in the middle of the city. I wondered if she was all right so I asked her. "I am one of those people" I said "who assist other people to cross the road only to find they don't want to get to the other side." It was lovely to hear her laughter mingled with my own. "I am waiting for someone" she said, "a friend is meeting me here." A woman in a wheelchair waiting on the corner, well why not. Comforting isn't it to realise that here was one person who despite everything was managing to live as normal a life as possible. It made me wonder whether if I were wheelchair bound I would have the courage to sit on a corner and wait for a friend. It would be comforting to believe that I would manage it but far more comforting to know that she actually could do it.

Once when travelling I stopped the car, got out and asked directions from a man in a wheelchair. The lady pushing him began to direct me. I looked at his sad eyes and crouched down beside him. "Could you explain?" He smiled and gave me full instructions. His wife who rules the wheelchair had forgotten in that instant the level of his capacity.

On speaking to a mother whose child was ill I asked if he was lying on the settee. She replied that yes he was. We know that, as children when feeling ill, it is good to lie on the settee. It's comforting to see mummy or daddy in the same room or to hear them close by pottering about in the kitchen. At times of sickness the bedroom is a million miles away. Even as adults we can feel isolated within our own discomfort in another part of the house. Have you ever thought to put a pillow lengthwise beside a sick child, have you appreciated how cosy it is for that child to lie next to that pillow to cuddle up, to keep warm and to feel comfortable and secure?

When something bad happens to us we often feel that no one cares or understands. Alone we sit amidst the whirlpool of doubt or even despair. Without comfort it is hard to survive the crisis. If we are lucky a friend or a caring relative puts out a hand and reaches into our despair, stopping us from being drawn completely in to the centre of our own doubt. The hand that metaphorically pulls us out provides support and in that support we are comforted.

My dentist is well over 6ft tall. He is a friendly giant with a heart made of marshmallow, a gentle touch and a belief in what he does. I am ashamed to say that I, despite all his kindness and his professionalism, am afraid when I visit him. Shaking I make my way to the chair and listen to his reassuring words and bathe in his kindness. A few days ago whilst sitting there he asked me if I was all right. I was not all right. In fact, I felt really dreadful. The last place that I wanted to be was in the dentist's chair. My emotional baggage, my own troubles, I had carried into the room with me, nothing really to do with my teeth. He talked to me and asked me what was making me look so tired and sad. He listened to what I had to say and there in that most unlikely of places I found so much comfort and solace that I was renewed. This man has a choice about the way he behaves, he can be a good dentist who looks after teeth or he can be a good dentist who cares passionately about the well being of his patients which includes looking after their teeth. So I came to the conclusion that my shaking and trepidation did not do very much for him. This man makes choices, his choices are comforting to others. He helps his patients to feel positive about themselves.

That day as I listened to his wise, helpful words my teeth were attended to only after my heart had been warmed by his kindness.

Tenderness and Kindness
are not signs of weakness and despair
but manifestations of
strength and resolution

Kahil Gibran

Often we hear the phrase "comfort" eating or "comfort" drinking, suggesting that people eat or drink to comfort themselves. Of course this is often the case. Feeling 'down' we pass the inviting windows of the bakery. The smell of newly baked bread assails our nostrils and we feel our mouths watering. Just a step or two and we are within the warm portals of this treasure house of mouth watering delicacies. Who can be blamed for comfort eating? There is a time and a place for most things.

Self comforting is an important part of our lives. We need to know how to make ourselves feel comfortable.

When we are small children we often know instinctively about self comforting. It is as adults that many of us find this whole process difficult.

Observe the baby in the pram. The small baby. Sleeping between meals. He awakens, small though he is he knows enough instinctively to form his hand into a tight little fist to push inside his mouth. "Expression" say the experts, "need it" the child would say if he were old enough to speak. See the toddling child, thumb in mouth, sucking away. "Nipple substitute" yell the experts, "like it" says the child. Observe the older child, usually competent, yet see him on a bad day when everything has gone wrong. Hand to mouth he bites his fingernails. "Body language" say the experts, "natural" says the child.

How can we continue to comfort ourselves? We can start by looking after or caring for what we have got. Now I don't want to talk about diets. Health centres and bookshops are full of them. However it is a known fact that caffeine really is not good for us. I expect my clients to drink decaffeinated coffee or tea. Of course I know that they may please themselves about what they will or will not choose to do, but the suggestion is made to them together with several others. Having refrained from caffeine intake they return with clearer eyes and a less dulled expression.

Because my clients are full to the brim with anxiety I suggest to them that they drink plenty of clear water. At first they look at me incredulously, wondering what I am suggesting. I try to make it easier for them by saying that an orange, unpeeled, sliced thinly, placed in a bottom of a jug, cold water poured upon it will enhance the taste of the water especially if on a hot day it has been in the fridge. I coax them into replacing at least one or two cups of tea or coffee a day with clear water, suggesting also that in doing so it will clear their system. Again it is true that when we feel anxious we find ourselves needing to go to the toilet more often. Passing fluid from our system often happens when we are overworked, overtired and overstretched. To aid this process, the passing through the system of clear water definitely helps — it is a caffeine free process.

Though not a vegetarian by nature, I am aware that when we are anxious it is much harder for our bodies to digest the protein in red meat. I recommend to my clients that they take red meat out of their diet. This need not be a permanent action, just something that is part of self comforting, after all to comfort ourselves we need to be in control of at least some of our bodily functions.

In this day and age a great many people get up in the morning and have a quick shower. Showers are extremely invigorating. You could say they are more invigorating than relaxing. Try after a hard day to cherish yourself. Run a deep warm bath, add your favourite bath balm or bubbles or gentle inexpensive soap. Place your towels within easy reach, remember this is 'deep treat time' then choose your favourite beverage and place it on the side of the bath. If you are alone in the house, your favourite tape or CD or indeed the radio playing in a nearby room within earshot could well give you further comfort or you may prefer to firmly close the door of the bathroom. Try hard not to use this time to think about all the chores that you need to do or everything that you think is going wrong in your life, all the negative aspects of your existence. Simply relax, imagine you are in a safe cocoon where no one can harm you.

Often busy mothers tell me they cannot bathe in this way. They are too busy. I suggest that they take a twenty minute slot out of their life each day even if this means that they get up earlier. It works, it puts something back into the system and is a part of the day that can never be taken away once experienced. This cherishing relaxation gives the anxious mum the belief that she still matters, but she has to believe in herself that she has a right to be cherished. After a hard day, feeling tired and weary, we are often not at our best. Small crises come and go in our lives, often diminishing our sense of well being. Deep baths are not magical but they do make spaces in our lives. To simply change ourselves is to find ways to survive.

People with small families often need the help of their partner or someone else in the family to allow them time to do something which will recharge the batteries. Husbands, partners if allowed and persuaded may well look after the family whilst the mother enjoys a long soak. How easy it is to feel guilty about doing this. Cries of "oh, I should be doing other things" reverberate through the house to say nothing of "there isn't time." Surely life should not just be about survival or existence. What about living? If your life is about survival or indeed you are merely existing, inject something else into your own scenario. Ask yourself what you need to do to really live your life. Who was it that said "we only have one life, this is not a rehearsal." This time on earth is the only time which we can be sure of. There are a great many people who believe themselves to be sure of another existence, another lifetime. It must be extremely comforting to be able to know that this is the case. Alas for many this is not so, all the more reason for making this life have a great deal of quality.

Self comforting takes us into many areas so let me say something about holidays. How often have you been on a holiday, having spent weeks looking forward to the day that you will set off on your journey,only to find that on arrival you have arranged such a busy schedule that you know without doubt that this holiday period will be tiring.

Ask yourself why you would do this in the first place, who were you trying to please, was it your partner, your wife, your children, was the holiday to be some sort of antidote to make everything right? Were your plans discussed together so that you were aware before your departure that it was going to be an exhausting time? Why did you arrange the holiday in this way? Sometimes people returning from holiday wished they had stayed at home.

Holidays need to be about relaxation in whatever form suits us. For one person pottering around archaeological remains can be extremely relaxing as can a visit to a museum. To another person this could be viewed as 'super' boring. For many rambling, donkey rides, horse riding, beach lying, sun soaking, canoeing, ski-ing have their place. The next time you book a holiday ask yourself what you intend to do. Someone once said to me "oh when we are on holiday we just do whatever comes into our heads." He was already extremely anxious worrying about every small thing. Because he was suffering from a condition of extreme anxiety and would get tired much more easily and probably needed to rest much more often, I suggested to him that some small plans might be appropriate. He gave me a strange reply "oh" he said "there are always hidden agendas to our holidays." When I spoke to him on his return he was absolutely exhausted. His condition had deteriorated and he was more anxious than ever. What was worse was the fact that his wife was now very angry with him. "He doesn't have any energy," she said, "none whatsoever."

I am not suggesting that it is necessary to sit still for a whole week or a fortnight, how boring that could be. What I am suggesting is that holidays planned from the first day you arrive often work out very well, especially if some wise person is saying we can't do that, we will be absolutely shattered! Make sure that when you are planning a holiday it is a holiday, not a time into which you have packed so many activities that the thought of them makes you feel exhausted.

Have you ever watched a hamster in his wheel? Imagine yourself as a hamster, going round and round in the wheel of life. Hamsters usually are quite sensible, when they feel tired they stop the wheel, they get out, snuggle into their little nest and go to sleep. How often do you stop the hamster wheel of life and get out? Imagine being a hamster who couldn't get out of the wheel, who drove it so fast that you became heady with the speed of it and thus eventually lost control. It shouldn't be necessary for you to depend on another person to lift you out of the hamster wheel, to tell you reassuringly that it is all right to stop, that it is allowable. If you are to care about yourself and your level of self comforting, then you need to have the ability to give yourself permission, as appropriate, to stop the wheel from going round.

Retirement can be a difficult time for many people. I am always worried when I speak to people in the last year of their working life who say "my work is every-thing, I do not know how I will cope." Pre-retirement courses help I'm sure as does advice from friends. For this person the hamster wheel and the driving of the wheel have been more important than the time spent warmly in the nest. Hamsters usually get it right, time in the nest, time in the wheel, look at your life, are you having enough time in the nest?

When anxious we often have problems with our digestion. This is due to the fact that food is eaten quickly and consequently the old digestive system finds itself in difficulties. Many of my clients feel totally fazed out by food while well meaning partners take them to restaurants only to find that half way through the meal the person is overwrought and even more anxious. Small quantities make a difference. The mind and body will not baulk at an amount of food upon the plate which look as though it can be coped with. If you are looking after someone who is suffering from anxiety and high levels of stress remember that a small amount of food nicely presented on a small plate will be much more acceptable than a Sunday roast dinner.

Self comforting is also about giving yourself time. Could you honestly say that in every 24 hour period of your life you sit quietly in a chair for 20 minutes, say to yourself this is my island, this is my space.

One lady when we discussed this said "oh I can't relax." "Do you ever try to sit still?" I asked. "Oh yes" she replied "I sit still saying I must do this, I must do that, I shouldn't be here" so she continued. It was only after her husband had left her together with a note which said "I cannot live with your obsessional cleanliness" that she realised they had not had an easy life together.

This lady hoped her husband would return — however years of the non-resting cleanliness regime had tired him out.

Take time out.

Take time to plan.

Take time to reflect.

Take time to love.

Above all take time to 'be' not only for yourself but for the benefit of others.

A hot bath! I cry, as I sit down in it; and again, as I lie flat, a hot bath! How exquisite a vespertine pleasure, how luxurious, fervid and flagrant a consolation for the rigours, the austerities, the renunciations of the day.

Rose Macaulay

There is no duty we so much
Underrate as the duty
of being happy.

Robert Louis Stevenson

Golden Days

My work involves quite a lot of travelling, and recently I stopped on the road in a busy town. The lollipop lady, outsize lolly in hand, ushered a group of small children across the road. Two boys jostled each other, laughed raucously and meandered out of line.

She spoke gently to them at first, and then she yelled at them. The bigger boy dug the smaller boy in the ribs, as they almost fell over themselves laughing. Their mirth was contagious, even the lollipop lady couldn't keep a straight face. I smiled too, as I waited in the car and thought of some of my yesterdays.

Strange how our yesterdays can so easily affect our todays and sometimes even our tomorrows — expected but not yet experienced. When my children were very young, we were a struggling little family — first mortgage, sessional work for me. The demands of every day living were a force to be reckoned with, and making ends meet became our prime concern — that was, if my children were to brought up in the manner I thought was right. This meant that frugality was really the order of the day.

At that time, I think I could have written a book entitled "Forty ways with Mince". I had a friend who always referred to me as the casserole queen but you see it was about managing. I didn't want us to be miserable. I didn't want the children to remember mum who went on and on about money or, really, went on and on about the lack of it. So one day, I packed a picnic lunch and took a cheap day ticket to the seaside and there we were on the coast, one baby boy slung across me in the baby carrier and the other two years and a bit toddling by my side.

I talked to them both of Golden Days. We stood at the edge of the sea and dug our toes into the wet sand. "This is a golden day" I said. The baby nuzzled in closer. He at that time had no comprehension whatsoever about what was a golden day. However, undaunted, I continued. "This is a golden day because we have the sea, the sun, the sand — all things that we can't have every day at home but they are ours today." We sat down on the beach. Nick, my toddler, was fidgeting and curious whilst Jonathan was a roly-poly of a baby, who liked to snuggle all the time — well, not quite all the time, because a great deal of the time, when he wasn't snuggling he was crying or even yelling according to the needs of the moment. "Golden Days" I continued "are to be experienced and stored. We drink them in." The only thing that the baby was drinking in at that moment was sand because, by this time, I had taken him out of the carrier seat and he had managed to roll over onto his tummy and was pushing quantities of sand into his mouth, rather indelicately.

Nick looked at me with still eyes. "Close your eyes darling" I said "Try to make a picture." So he and I did. We held his brother between us and we closed our eyes trying to preserve the sound of the gulls, the noise of the people on the beach, the ripple of the waves, the smell of the air and the way the sun felt because it warmed our bodies.

I feel, and I felt then, that perhaps all people have a right to golden days. They can take place anywhere really. My children's lives were dotted with golden days — not measured in monetary terms — they weren't about expense or cost but they were really measured in love and experience, just like the day at the steam rally.

As an adult, I had no idea whatsoever what magic steam could conjure up. All that power, all that effort, could it be responsible for producing music, movement and magic. Had I lived in ignorance for so long? At an early age, I was taught to appreciate the theatre and art. I have always been grateful to the parents who took me constantly to new musicals, plays — in fact everything that was going. What a gift to give a growing child. Some of my golden days as a child happened in the theatre. Once, I saw George Formby at the Palace Theatre in Manchester. I didn't think he had much of a voice, but his personality . . . oh! and I loved his cheeky grin. We all need golden days so that we can store them away in our memory and then, when life is particularly grim, we can wander off — we can think again about the good days that we had. I can hear the cynics saying "Golden Days won't sort our problems". But you know, the child who has never known a golden day, who has never been shown love, often does not know how to love because that child has very little in their emotional bank.

Once, whilst working with a group of very disturbed teenagers, I met a girl called Jenny. The first time we were introduced, how she fought and kicked and sought only to hurt me and, in fact, anyone else who happened to get close to her. She said in a loud voice that she hated me and that she hadn't met people like me before and she hoped she would never meet any more! I assured her that very probably she hadn't. As she bit and scratched and struggled, I asked her a question "Have you ever had a golden day?"

Panting, ducking and weaving with her arms flailing around, her answer was a stream of expletives. She thought I was crazy. Of course, she never had a golden day. I knew that but later, much later, I was to teach her how to go out and make them happen.

Fourteen years later, she came to see me with her husband and her own tiny baby. She had gone to a great deal of trouble to find me after ten years. What an emotional reunion it was and I felt love welling up in my heart for her and for her little family. Her eyes held mine as she said "one day I met him." She turned and touched her husband's face and do you know, it was a golden day. The day we all had together, was another. I nursed the baby and I watched Jenny and her husband enjoying the pleasure of simply being together, having made the journey to meet an old friend. Before they left, Jenny said "I had to find you — I needed to tell you that now I understand about golden days and that my little one is going to have golden days because I'm going to make them happen for her." It had taken her fourteen years to really understand and ten years to find me again.

As I waved them goodbye, and watched them rattle off in their old banger of a car, I thought of the girl, the flailing arms and the swearing lips, the moving body and the stringy hair and the foul mouth but who now knew about golden days.

Just occasionally in our lives, we are very lucky, because someone makes the journey back across the years to share a special something with us and then of course, that makes yet another golden day. Do you have golden days? Days that really matter. Days that you can treasure and preserve and carefully store away and place in your emotional bank account.

When someone we love leaves us, when a child marries and walks away, when a husband chooses someone else, when we seem to fail at everything we attempt, then golden days really do begin to matter. They don't make everything all right, but they can be taken out from the memory box and lived again and again and sometimes they give us a small amount of confidence in the future because they record happiness experienced in the past.

Once, I was privileged enough to meet and spend time with a man who had been a prisoner in a concentration camp during World War II. Over a long period of time, he talked to me quite calmly of his experiences. I was so intrigued by what he had to say, that I decided to find out about how people survived and what had kept them going through those terrible, terrible days and, as a result, I eventually spoke to about twenty people who had all had a similar experience. Some had been prisoners of war in Germany. One man even talked to me of being imprisoned in Siberia in the thirties. What terrible true stories they had to tell.

Sometimes, I cried with them and sometimes I unashamedly showed my love for them as they related the pain and suffering. One man's words will live in my mind forever. He said "those who survived best were not necessarily those who had the will to live or those who were the most courageous, or even those who were the strongest. The true survivors were the dreamers. Those who, despite the cruel, harsh reality in which they existed, held in their minds a picture so vivid, so glorious, so happy and joyous that they stayed alive to have the experience again." Almost all of them he said "thought of a particular place or a particular person and as for me" he continued "when things were at their worst, I thought of my mother's Sussex garden. I saw her in her blue apron, I could smell the bread rising on the oven top, and even when I thought I would die, when I thought I should die, somehow, that picture, that memory lived on and with it so did I."

He had lived on, for there we were, together, talking about golden days. Some of my most memorable golden days have been spent out in the country. I like to escape with those I love, friends and family — away from it all, where we can treasure the still beauty of old mother nature and after we have drunk our fill, we make the weary journey back to town. There are golden hours to be had and even golden moments too.

A friend of mine told me of a special golden moment. Her mother had died after a long stay in hospital. Some months before her death, she had ceased to be able to recognise my friend and although she was chirpy enough, her mind was obviously engaged elsewhere but after her death one of the nurses on the ward said "you know, your mother seemed to blossom every time you came, it seemed such a small matter that she couldn't even remember your name because you made her smile so much."

Some people let the golden moments and the golden hours pass them by. They feel it takes too much effort to grasp them and keep them. Or perhaps they are unwise enough to believe that if they elude us once, they will evade us forever.

Once at Christmas time, during a midnight service in my local church, everyone's head bowed low, at a particular place in the service, like a naughty schoolgirl I looked up, as I had so many times before, at all the bowed heads and I could remember back across the years having done this from about four years of age, peeping out, looking and seeing but this particular night, how lucky it was that I did because you see, I saw the face of a toddler, glowing in the candlelight.

He was perched on his father's shoulder and his eyes were full of wonder as he viewed all the adults around him bowing before an unseen God. What I saw in his little face wasn't only wonder but love and security and just to prove to me that that was exactly what his message was about he snuggled deeper into his daddy's neck. The wonder of the crib was there for him to see, the flickering candles, the music, the bowed heads of the adults, all of this in his small world. He did not know that he was having a golden moment, he did not know that at sometime in the future it would be possible that he could remember some of the fleeting glimpses of that night, that special magical Christmas night. When he is older and he recalls he will remember the warmth of daddy's neck and the feeling and the knowing that it was all right just to be himself and to be there, a golden moment indeed.

Golden moments. Don't let them pass you by.

When did you last share a special golden day with a friend? Someone that you love and cherish. When did you last put your hand out and reach and keep a golden moment and from this golden moment build a golden day?

A very special golden day began in the early hours of a spring morning some years ago. It began in a minibus in the middle of Liverpool. The passengers were ten teenagers. At sometime in their lives all of them had lived on the streets of Liverpool, had been helped by the various services, charities and through that help were now striving to manage with what was hopefully to be a better life. The minibus travelled in the early hours to the Lake District to a farmhouse especially chosen, rented to accommodate what I hoped would be the making of a Golden Day for these young people. The idea of this day had been born months beforehand whilst on a visit to Liverpool to do a particular piece of work. I had noticed a young boy on the streets who was obviously existing literally on the streets of Liverpool. It struck me very forcibly at that time how lucky I was that I did not need to be earning my living on a street somewhere. I began to wonder if this boy had ever seen a green field or watched the sun rise.

On that spring morning the bus stopped outside the front door of the farmhouse. With great trepidation the youngsters disembarked. Walking wearily with their helper who was also the driver they eyed not only me but their surroundings with worry, anxiety, fear and trepidation. Smiling I tried to reassure them, believing that it was possible to assist these young people to appreciate the finer things in life. In order to help me to bring about this minor miracle, I had enlisted the help of eight police officers all of whom had given up a day of their rest time, holidays, whatever. They were willing to spend time in the company of young people who had usually seen the police as enemies. Today was different however as the youngsters did not know that these jovial strong characters who helped them through a day in the country were really the people they so despised.

Walks in the woods were arranged with instructions to return for a farmhouse lunch, a boat trip across the lake for some, a trek round the road for others, all on a one to one basis.

Then it happened, a shout from the woods across the road, a crashing of branches, a tumbling jumbling of booted feet one after the other and eventually almost landing from space in my kitchen was Gary. "You liar, you liar" he shouted into my face, "you liar". "Do you mean me?" I asked. "You're a liar" he shouted again. Soon his partner, his helper joined us in the kitchen, a man in his late thirties with 15 years' police experience. A man respected and admired by his colleagues and also respected by me. "Sorry about this" he said "I had to tell him I couldn't lie."

It transpired that during their walk Gary had asked what Peter did for a living. Through all our well designed plans we had foolishly not considered this eventuality. At that moment Gary began to smash the crockery in the kitchen, banging into cupboard doors, stamping his feet, telling me repeatedly that I was a liar and that Peter was nothing but a pig. I said "enough is enough" but through it all Peter stood rock still and solid, never taking his eyes off Gary. Not a muscle moved.

I tried to explain and then through the open kitchen door totally uninvited there entered a big woolly sheep. A woolly sheep making the noises that sheep usually make. Suddenly the scene was changed. It was Gary who now stood rock still. It was as though he was transfixed with fear. At that moment both Peter and I began to move simultaneously as we realised that this boy was absolutely terrified of the animal. As we moved so the sheep moved towards him. He backed against the kitchen door and began to shake from head to toe. Crying, he screamed out "don't let it near me, don't let it near me." Before we could say anything everything happened so quickly. He sank to the floor and became a huddled weeping mass. As I tried to shoo the unwanted sheep out of the door I saw Peter crouch down making himself a shield between Gary and the rest of the room. The animal was not for leaving however and began to race round the kitchen, obviously afraid itself in its unfamiliar surroundings. As it passed by Peter and Gary the boy shrieked even louder and Peter, bending closer to him, placed his arms about him and held him close. Gary accepted the comfort, a comfort given probably for the first time in his life. A golden moment that might never ever have occurred. Having closed the outer door I looked at man and boy and tears filled my eyes, the brash boy who had called me a liar was now a small boy sitting on a man's knee, crumpled, dishevelled and afraid whilst a big caring gentle giant hugged him and gave him not only comfort but protection.

Ten years later Peter and Gary are still in touch and it is true that Gary's life has not suddenly become totally full of Golden Days — but at least he has one friend to whom he can still turn.

Golden moments, don't let them pass you by! When did you take the chance to give someone sixty minutes of a golden hour? It's sad how often we value time and people in retrospect. We start our sentences with "If only I'd done more for him before . . ."

"Before what?" you might ask. "Before it was too late" would be the answer.

Go out — give yourself and others a golden time!!

Seize the day

A gift consists not in what
is done or given, but in
the intention of the giver or doer.

Seneca

Trust

The dictionary tells us that trust means belief in or reliance on a personal thing. It is a duty, a responsibility one feels bound to fulfil.

How many people in your life at the present moment do you feel you could trust implicitly? People you believe in, people you rely on? If you are one of life's lucky people you will be able to reply father, mother, brother, sister, wife, husband, children, friends, note the plural of the word friend. However, for some people this is not the case. They are not so lucky. You may be in that category. Reading and thinking "who can I trust?" and then rethinking, finding the list to be quite small. People who are hurt during their childhood often learn to mistrust the words and the actions of others. Coaxed, reassured and loved as adults they sometimes heal sufficiently to trust again.

Babies are for loving. They come into the world as trusting little people. If the adults in whom they trust hurt them then as they grow they do not know whom to trust. Emotionally they become deprived unless they are lucky enough to learn to trust a person or a thing. Something starts to help them to believe once more in what the whole process of trusting is about. David had a dog. A mongrel. "What else?" he once said. "What other kind of dog would want to be with me, and no one wanted him anyway. He was on death row at the dog's home, now he is mine. He is better than most of the people I know, asks for little, doesn't expect very much but most of all he is faithful, true to me. You should see his hackles rise when someone shouts at me." David smiles. David, born free, lonely by the time he was 12 months old. Unwanted, left crawling on a beach. Mother unfit, father unknown. Children's homes, scores of them. Self mutilating, teenage years with institutional tattoos.

"The dog doesn't mind" he says. Then into David's life came Ben. Ben the man. Rough, tough, no wimp. Ready to give David just a small chance. No sympathy, just a chance. He trusted David to work with him in his small factory making wrought iron goods. David lived in. For three months David grew in the family and began, it seemed, to trust other human beings. Then one day he ran away taking tools and money with him. Ben's tools. Ben's wife Helen owned the money.

Ben said if he caught David he would beat him within an inch of his life. Ben sought and found David. He didn't beat him. He ranted and raved, cuffed him a bit and brought him back to the little factory and the house. "You live here" he bawled, "you bloody well live here. Get it, this is your home, your home, don't blow it lad, trust us for Pete's sake, trust us." David truculently replied "Whose Pete? You're a liar anyway, you don't want me."

Next day Ben took David to the Dog's Home. He said choose. If you can't trust people then trust one of these. David, afraid, wanted to go out of the place. The whining of the dogs made him even more afraid. He felt sorry for them. He felt like one of them and he wanted to set them all free. He knew that he couldn't and didn't want to be there. Ben, wise, said "this is where they come to die, rescue one for God's sake, rescue one" and there in the Dog's Home David didn't say "whose God?"

David couldn't think of a name for the dog. He thought of Bruce, Dart, Speed or Grass. David thought he'd watch their faces when he suggested he'd call his dog Grass. "Trust" said Helen "or Hope". "Can't call a dog Hope" said Ben. Big rough wise Ben. David agreed. Trust loved David, he still does. David loves Trust and Ben and Helen and now he even believes that some of the customers coming into the workshop like him too. Well just a bit he thinks. It's easier to get on with people when you have got a dog says David and everyone loves my Trust.

Many people who come to see me go home to empty houses, no one to ask how their day went, no one to show them affection, no one to trust. A cat, though having a mind of its own and wanting to go out whenever it wills, will often be there to push and rub itself against your legs. A rabbit in a hutch in a garden can be another source of comfort. A dog though is your friend. You can stroke a dog, talk to him, teach him. Unlike a cat who will decide that this or that is appropriate, a dog can be coerced and loved into doing what he is told. He needs a firm hand, a firm voice and a lot of unbroken promises. As Ben said to David "if you can't trust people then maybe you should think of something else."

Where trust is firmly in place forgiveness often comes quite easily. Trust within the friendship ensures that even when things go wrong the trust will hold the friends together. One friend will say of another I am sure she didn't really mean to hurt me and be of the understanding that this is so. In trust we can be honest. In trust we can say that it wasn't quite right. Without trust none of this is possible. Without trust the same sentences sound like a criticism. "Do you know how much you have hurt me" can be a condemnation. "Do you know how much you have hurt me" when there is enough trust will evoke in the other friend a feeling of remorse or there will be a need for explanation.

Trust is so important in life. The child toddling who looks at you and holds out an out—stretched palm so that you can take it in yours and lead him where he needs to be. Trust is invaluable in life. "How many people in your life do you trust?" was the question I asked at the very beginning of this piece. Now I ask "how many people trust you?" and if there are so few that you have to think really hard then ask yourself what you will do in the days and weeks and months to come to ensure that more people do trust you. Send out those positive messages that suggest that you will be without destructive criticism, you can be given information and you keep it a secret. Think again how many people you trust. How many people trust you.

On Being Extra ... ordinary

Some people by their very being improve and enrich the quality of life for others. The people I am to tell you about in the next 43 pages now have enriched my life and comforted me greatly.

Have you ever read of the experiences of a particular person? Their trials and tribulations, their triumphs and their continued strength. If on reading you have felt refreshed and restored, if your faith in human kind has been strengthened then you will know exactly what I mean. Restored faith is often very comforting.

When I was a small child in the infant school I loved to tell stories. My classmates listened as I embellished verbal adventures of various people who were really just figments of my imagination.

Soon a particular teacher realised that I had a certain talent. In those early days I don't think there was even a chance that she thought I might one day write successfully. She merely grasped that I had a talent for capturing the attention of other children and keeping them quiet. As a consequence whenever there was a staff meeting I was asked to look after the class. Sitting in front of them I would tell them an interesting story. It was always a kind of cliff-hanger because whenever I heard the teachers returning up the corridor I would put in a very quick point and leave my listeners on the edge of their seats, with the words 'I'll finish it next time.' Somehow or other when next time came I couldn't remember just where I'd left the character and another cliff-hanger would begin.

One of the characters in my stories was called Selina Silver. I described her as a small china ornament looking rather like a little Dutch girl. I had seen pictures of Dutch girls and knew what they looked like in their aprons, clogs and hats. Selina Silver in my story lived in the third drawer of a bureau. She was put there because she was slightly chipped and the family did not want her to be seen by everyone because she was damaged. However they couldn't throw her away because she had been a present from a rich great aunt.

My classmates loved the adventures of Selina Silver, there was so much that she managed to get up to. There were other characters too, like Melissa the Mermaid and also the Magical Flying Lady. By the time I was twelve my story telling knew no bounds and I decided that that was what I wanted to be when I grew up — a story teller. Today, on the shelf near my bed together with books and other bits and pieces is a china ornament, a little Dutch girl. I'd like to tell you how this ornament came into my life.

My dream of producing children's stories continued. I wanted to capture the imagination of little ones giving them some escape or relief from what the world had to offer. A little touch of fantasy and magic that would always help children think of other happier events. However, publishers turned my stories down and rejection slips became part of my life. I was working as a counsellor at the time when into my life came Joey. Joey was 27 and I was asked if I would counsel him. He had had what he described as a nervous breakdown. There was a 'dour' look about him, very little eye contact and his shoulders were constantly hunched, hands folded tightly across his chest or clasped in front of him. He felt a great need to sit on one side of my desk while I sat at the other. If I moved he moved further away. He spurned the comfortable easy chairs offered and resolutely sat himself down where he thought he should be. Although he didn't tell me so I realised that he needed me always to sit behind my desk. Definitely not my practise as a counsellor. The first sessions came and passed, there was no response, no speech from him, not even a flicker and then a breakthrough when he agreed to have a cup of tea and a biscuit. Without really knowing why I said "what we both need Joey is a bit of magic, a bit of the old Selina Silver." His head moved ever so slightly. Silence.

Another session came and went and then unexpectedly he uttered one word "magic" to which I replied "Selina Silver." I talked to him about this little character. I drew her on a piece of paper at my desk. There was little response from Joey but I knew that he liked the drawing and I asked him if he would like to take it with him when the session was over. He nodded. He took the paper, carefully folded it until it was an inch square, and put it in his top pocket.

Week by week our sessions continued getting nowhere going nowhere, no journeying for this young man and I. Then one day he brought the piece of paper back and unfolded it in front of me. "Tell me" he said, "tell me." So I did. I told him about the infant school and about the stories and my dreams. This meant that I had to break all my own counselling rules for never before had I said "I" to any client, but I felt that he was different and, as he had asked a direct question, I needed as always to be truthful and to try to keep his confidence.

It was obvious that he took great pleasure in hearing about this little character Selina Silver. I began to tell him stories. At first he rocked then he crooned and then for the first time there was a little eye contact and Joey and I began our long journey together. We journeyed through the forest of misunderstanding. We needed to step carefully through the fantasies, fears and everything else that was in his mind so that I could learn where his terrible pain had really begun. Eventually in exchange for my stories he told me his. Unlike mine that were made up and fiction, his story was true and painful. He talked of being a soldier and how much he had wanted to be a soldier. His mother's pride and belief in him and the sparkle it had put into his life, and then he had been sent to Northern Ireland. Patrols sometimes didn't return and many soldiers were injured. Injury after injury, shooting after shooting and then to Joey it was as though the bottom had fallen out of his world and nothing else mattered. He began to be irritable and resented any show of affection. When he returned home on leave he could not bear to be in a room with those who said they loved him, and in order to keep himself safe and separate he exhibited anger the like of which his family had never seen.

One day whilst in Ireland he was the only survivor when a group of soldiers were attacked. Everyone else was left for dead but he for some reason remained intact. From that day on he had never ever forgiven himself for being alive. Retreating into a world of total silence he had tried hard to exist without living. During the time that we spent together Joey cried a great deal. Somewhere in his heart he had to find a way to forgive himself for the fact that he had survived while those with whom he had served had died. He could not forgive himself for surviving. It made him feel worthless and he talked in depth about the gifts and talents of his comrades. Eventually he screamed at me "I wished I had died with them, there is no life without them." In time Joey's emotional wounds healed. He began carefully and slowly to build a new life, a life in education where he could help to mould the lives and thoughts and dreams of students. He said he felt shriven, that the terrible pain had started to heal. He was able to say that at last he forgave himself.

The day came for us to say goodbye. He wanted to give me a hug and I was glad to be hugged by Joey. We had travelled a long way together. Several weeks later whilst preparing to move house, head deep inside yet another tea chest, the doorbell rang. A moan escaped me. Who could this be? And on this day of all days. I really didn't want to know. Shouting vainly for someone else in the family to open the door I realised that my house was full of deaf ears. Therefore it was I who opened the door. Standing on the step was Joey, smart, well dressed. "Hello" he said "I've brought you a present." Without more ado he thrust a small box into my hand and then before I could say anything at all he ran off down the path. I wanted to run after him to say come in, look at the chaos, have a cup of tea but I knew instinctively that that was not the right thing to do.

Reaching the gate he turned and waved and I waved back. Carefully I opened the box and as I unwrapped the fine tissue paper my tears fell abundantly onto my apron and onto the contents of the box. For there inside a velvet nest was a pottery model of the Selina Silver that I had drawn for Joey during one of his early sessions with me. This Selina Silver was exactly as I had described. Every colour perfect, every detail. Now she sits proudly on the bookshelves in my bedroom.

Joey is long gone out into the world and I have never heard from him since nor do I need to for part of him is always with me whilst he has gone on to do much greater things. Joey is an example of what extraordinary people are about. He had been to the bottom of the pit and from that stance had seen the sun rise behind the mountain. It was a privilege for me to work with him and be allowed to help him to know himself. I hope you will find some comfort in Joey's story and as for you Joey I hope you read this book and wherever you are I know that you will recognise yourself. Thank you for helping me to grow as a person and thank you for giving me a constant reminder that dreams can become substance, just like the drawing of Selina Silver.

For every hill I've had to climb

For every stone that bruised my feet,

For all the blood and sweat and grime

For blinding storms and burning heat

My heart sings but a grateful song

These were the things that made me strong!

Francis Gay, 1983

If I am going to write about being extraordinary I must tell you about Don.

The first time I met him we were speaking on the telephone about one of his clients who was also my client. A kindly man, Don was a GP in what can only be described as a cosmopolitan area. Within the mixed and varied population he sought not only through his medical practice, but through his everyday life, to make all men equal. White, black, black, white, or whatever creed or persuasion. He was appalled by cruelty and prejudice. His requirement and expectation of others was that they love one another as he did. He was tireless in his efforts to bring about a community in which all could live safely. His telephone rang constantly whilst he responded with whatever help he could. A Christian without being in any way bigoted who presented Christianity in such a form that even the most seasoned and hardened atheist felt compelled to listen to what this great man had to say. Within his greatness there was also humility for he never ever took the credit for his own actions. Believing them to only be possible because of God.

In order for Don to continue to be extraordinary he needed Carol, Carol his wife who when he was tired, like Aaron with Moses held up his arms for all to see so that he could continue with the work that pleased his soul. And then one day Don was gone, taken, dead. No more to be seen, at least not in this life. A favourite walk in the Lakes, a stumble, a slip, a roaring for a few yards and death. The world robbed of a gem so vibrant and precious that in his place only dullness can remain. But Don's efforts and his beliefs continued to be upheld by the community in which he lived, by his family and friends who will never let his memory die. His kindness to me was immeasurable, to spend an hour with Don was to be filled with a feeling of such immense comfort. He lifted every burden from those he met who sought his help.

O, free my weary eyes from tears,
Or close them fast in death!
But, if I must afflicted be,
to suit some wise design;
Then man my soul with firm resolves,
To bear and not repine!

Robert Burns

And then there was Hunter, now Hunter really was extraordinary. With a name like Hunter how could he be anything else? I couldn't believe that it was his Christian name. I thought it had to be his surname but no he said it was a family name and that was his first name — Hunter. Hunter was amazing. I met him in the most unlikely place, namely the hospice. People often think that hospices are not very uplifting places and see them mainly as where people actually go to die but this was not the case here.

Hunter was enduring a great deal of pain and as a consequence needed help coping with that pain. As is usual with visualisation therapy the patient is required to imagine their own cancer or disease and has to establish and imagine of what they see that cancer to be. Many people suffering from cancer describe a purple mountain, others a jellylike amoeba. Hunter saw his cancer as a mountain. So he and I talked of recruiting and establishing an imaginary army that he could conjure up in his mind. He was to equip the army with all sorts of weapons and to imagine that his army of soldiers went towards the purple mountain with the distinct intention of destroying it. Hunter liked this idea. It pleased him and despite his pain he entered wholeheartedly into the fantasy.

The next time I saw him he had written out a long list of the people in his army. At the top of his list was Mickey Mouse. When I looked questionably at this he said "well the troops, the soldiers, need to be entertained!" Further down amongst the names of his friends was the name Jesus Christ. How did he get in there I asked. "Well," he said "Mickey Mouse to entertain them and Jesus Christ knows all about suffering so he can help them, pick them up when they are down, assist them, you know what I mean". Further down the list in a separate space was my name. "I am no soldier" I said. "No" he said "you are separate from the others, you are the Captain, you are in charge of the army that is going to fight the purple mountain. Your army and my army are going to make sure that this cancer doesn't kill me."

As I drove home I didn't feel like an army captain, in fact I didn't feel a whole person. I felt as though I had been presented through my own work with a situation with which I couldn't cope but I did cope. I coped because of Hunter. You see, what he insisted on doing despite his terrible illness, he insisted on visiting a large book store. With the help of staff and relatives he managed to stand in this store and buy me a book. A book of Robert Burns' poetry. When he presented me with the book I couldn't believe that he had actually managed to get out of his bed at the hospice, put up with his pain, endure the hardship and actually buy the book. But he did. He talked to me about being English and not being able to understand the words of the great bard and to help me further he asked a friend or relative, I am not quite sure which, to bring him a Scottish Dictionary and this in turn was presented to me.

Towards the end Hunter and I made the pact that I make with all the people I meet through revisualisation, they are all quite clear that they do not want me at the funeral. I have tried to decide in my own mind why this is the case but feel that perhaps it is a question that should remain unanswered. Shortly before his death I spoke to him. By then his condition was extremely painful and he knew that he would soon die. "Permission to stand the army down please Captain" he said next time we spoke, "permission granted" said I and so it was. So Hunter's imaginary army of individuals went back from whence they came and the purple mountain that had grown and grown took Hunter for its own.

Before he died I promised Hunter that whenever I trained nurses in the future I would mention him, that I would tell them about the army and teach them about revisualisation because he said it had been a great help. From Hunter I learned about endurance, tolerance and most of all about a need to live, and I am greatly comforted whenever I think about Hunter. I try to remember on those days when I have grouched my way through the early hours because I think I feel ill or badly done to that Hunter, despite everything kept his army entertained, well looked after and put a Captain in charge. What greater comfort could there be.

Why not think about the extraordinary people in your life? They are there somewhere waiting to be used as examples. People whose lives may well give you comfort and help you to cope. Whenever I think of Mahatma Ghandi I remember the story about him when he was travelling in an open train and one of his pointed slippers accidentally slipped from his foot on to the track. Quick as a flash he pulled off the other slipper and threw it after the first. Master, said someone with him, now you have no shoes. Ghandi looked at his follower "what use is it for a man to find one shoe when he needs two, one shoe will be no use and no comfort at all."

I believe that comfort has many sources. We may believe that we are unable to find those sources. When we feel low and use or misuse the word depressed it is well to remember that this condition, in its non clinical sense, is one in which we can think only of ourselves, our shortcomings, our failings and everything that is not comforting. To seek comfort we need to step out from that spiral of personal distrust. Imagine the man finding Ghandi's two shoes. A pair, obtaining a useful aid to his walking. Remember my book from Hunter. I understand the work of Robert Burns much more. Remember Don and the human legacy that he has left behind in the people of his own district, remember Selina Silver who sits to remind me that life goes on.

"ALL THAT IS NOT GIVEN IS LOST."

Jean

One day I met Jean. Tired, weary and lacking confidence. Resting as best she could between the years of 50 and 60. No longer young, nor at the time of our meeting believing herself capable of ever feeling young again. Her eyes were tired, she carried her body like a great weight, sighs seemed to multiply within her and every few seconds sought their escape into the fresh air.

We walked in a garden tranquil in the sunshine. Coming upon a white bench we sat cornerwise at either end and looked at each other. She talked, she needed to talk, because she felt trapped and helpless.

For many weeks, or even months, she had not known where to turn. She told me of her life in Liverpool, of her children and beautiful grandchildren and at the mention of these, her little ones, her face glowed and I saw within it a hint or promise or was it even a remembrance of a Jean once known to herself and now believed lost.

Ten months before we met Jean had had major surgery and since that time had felt rather listless. Her doctors had provided little help so her lethargy and listlessness grew until it became an effort to do things as before. During these months her young daughter had given birth to a beautiful child, a little girl, a child so like the little girl lost to Jean when aged only four that Jean looking at her felt nothing but undying and abiding love.

We talked of the dead child, of the way she, Jean, had coped as a mother, taking on the years and then with great bravery deciding that life had to go on. Still vivid in her memory the empty words of a so called friend, I never thought she was meant for this world anyway, as though the little blue eyes and the long golden hair were the simple criteria to qualify for early death. In this new grandchild Jean was living again those four precious years.

Since the operation Jean had felt needs. Needs coming from within herself, needs she had never acknowledged before. She, the mother, the coper, the giver, now required to be 'as the child' herself. She needed to be cherished, to be loved. She reached out to her children, needing them to say "We'll look after you, we will take the worry, we understand".

So many needs this lady was experiencing. She had difficulty in remembering a time when she had not given and yet now, when we met, she could not see or even visualise her own personal strength, which to an outsider, even now, strained to be free from beneath the cloak of her weariness.

"I need them all to understand" she said, "to realise that I am not really strong. Sometimes I am so afraid but no one in the family seems to notice, they just think 'good old mum, she'll cope, mum always copes.' "Do you know" she went on "even when I got back from hospital friends, yes friends, not my family, my friends came to see me and asked how I was and then almost before I could answer they told me all about their own problems. I felt like screaming."

Of course she didn't. She lay in her bed, listening, advising and continued to be 'good old Jean'. The friends, then having rested their emotional burdens upon her, went more cheerfully on their way whilst Jean remained, feeling heavier for the weight of other people's problems.

"I didn't want it but what could I do, I couldn't say anything, they needed me."

How difficult it is for the rock to stand and say I may look strong, I may appear tough but if you dig through my exterior beyond my outer layers you will find that I am really soft marshmallow inside. Not totally impossible for the rock to say but almost unbelievable for those living with the rock.

Sometimes those who have leaned upon us, those who have benefited from our strength, those who have laid countless troubles at our door, are able to do this with ease because of the image we have. It is about the messages we give out. If we look upon a rock it looks strong. We believe we can stand upon it. We trust it to take our weight because its very appearance suggests it has qualities to do so.

If in the midst of bearing our weight it crumbles into a gooey mass then of course we feel disappointed, let down. It is as though the messages that the rock gave were false, untrue. The rock lied; leading us to believe in its strength and it is as though our belief and faith in it were just a figment of our imagination.

Now who wants to believe that, especially of a rock much loved and depended upon? Jean was obviously as that rock to her family, to her friends and acquaintances. Part of being strong in a family is about having power, mums have great power, they can change the attitude of a new generation or indeed destroy it altogether. Fathers play their part but somehow it is mothers that seem to tug at the heartstrings of their children much more effectively. They reach inside their hearts to pass on traditions, ways, but most of all, coping skills.

Children without this pattern, this learning process, have to cope in other ways, sometimes depending on street wisdom to help them through.

In the sunshine Jean and I talked. She had felt she was going mad when recently in the midst of typing out a document for a friend a thought had come into her head about a dream she had had. It was hard now to identify what it had all been about but her heart had pounded and she had felt uneasy, wanting to leave the typing and walk away into the fresh air and this she sensibly had done.

But being Jean, never having had an experience before over which she had little or no control she went to see her doctor, but he gave her little help at all. Having listened to her short description of this very small but frightening experience he immediately told her she would need to see a psychiatrist saying "this is out of my league, you will have to see a specialist."

Jean, coming from a strong working class background, felt the fingers of dread tighten round her heart. It palpitated more than it had done whilst she had been sitting at the typewriter, because this time there was a suggestion that her mind was unsound. How could she return to her family and tell them that she was to see a psychiatrist. The doctor suggested that her condition was so serious that she must go to the hospital immediately and get an appointment.

Still filled with dread, her steps dogged with fear and trepidation, she took the bus to the hospital and walking in to the psychiatric unit felt her whole life had collapsed. An appointment was made but it was for weeks hence, so she thought 'perhaps I am not as seriously ill as my doctor is suggesting, for surely, here, in this awful place, the experts can look and see madness in faces immediately'.

On returning home she told no one of her terrible experience but closed it within herself, remaining on the outside strong and rock-like. But deep inside her heart was the guilt and degradation of this new image or perception she now had of herself, I'm going mad.

Perhaps her Doctor was busy;
Perhaps he was tired himself;
Perhaps he liked to keep his hands clean;
Perhaps he believed that this woman was indeed on the edge of madness.

Here in the tranquil garden, if that were indeed the case, there were no signs of this madness. Just a tired, weary, human being, wrestling with a dreadful suggestion put to her by a man who she felt should know, simply because, after all he is a doctor.

It was then that Jean and I talked of a great ruler, well really it would be better to say that I talked and she listened.

Many years ago this great man heard his warriors speaking together. He had decided to visit his garrison and wearing an old cloak he had passed unrecognised amongst them. No one cares about us he heard them say, no one bothers if we are dead or alive, we are just numbers, dying or wounded we are expendable, we can be rubbed out just like a number. So saying one soldier traced a number in the dust at his feet with the toe of his sandal and then, with great vehemence, ground it out with his heel.

What do they care said one of his companions, up there, drinking wine, having their women, what do they care about us. When did they last smell battle or feel the warm trickle of blood down their face.

With his head down the great ruler left and returned to his sumptuous apartments. The luxury of his palace now so obviously different from the barren emptiness of the garrison.

That night he could not sleep, despite the wine he had copiously drunk before retiring. Into his mind came the images of his soldiers, their anguished faces but most of all their bitterness and cynicism. He thought long and hard until at last he had to admit that they were right. He had not smelt battle for over thirty years, how could he possibly know what his warriors felt, they were far from unjust when describing his involvement. He had become a man of letters, much manipulated by his advisors, agreeing to proposals and signing orders put before him with great ease, with little consideration for the consequence in terms of human life or suffering. When welcoming his blood stained warriors back to base he had not felt a tearing in his heart for those who could no longer tramp the homeward path.

So the following day he summoned forth those who sought to advise and manipulate him. He informed them that he would, himself, go to battle. They, believing themselves to have more power than was truly theirs, pooh-poohed his notion, thinking that it was just a thought and would pass. Soon however, they were to be disillusioned, when the ruler who they realised held the ultimate power prepared to do as he had said.

It was a terrible experience for him. In thirty years the battle scene had changed in so many ways and yet there was an odd familiarity about it. He soon noticed that the men in the front lines were left to fight for far too long, their leaders being reluctant to withdraw and re-form.

The ruler was appalled. Suddenly he knew why victory had cost so much in terms of life. It was as though the men in charge would rather watch the soldiers die than admit that a little ground could be lost at one time in order to be regained at another.

So leaving his safe place in the battle, where he was well guarded by men who would give their lives for him, he took over. A new pattern was formed with short bursts of fighting on the very front lines followed by a withdrawal and a resting period during which other soldiers replaced the original number. A time to fight, he thought, a time to recuperate and gather strength. A single warrior given a few moments to rest safely behind a rock could return and nobly fight again. Hitherto any warrior seeming to falter had been thought a coward and as a consequence forfeited his life. In this new order the ruler gave permission to rest and return.

His soldiers learned to love and respect the man who had left the luxury of his palace to see what their lives were about first hand. They did not need his sympathy, nor had they ever sought it. They had needed empathy. They had wanted this ruler, or someone with power, to stand in their shoes and look out at the world through their eyes.

When I had finished speaking Jean was very quiet. The garden remained as tranquil as ever. The sun shone, its warmth bathing us. The moment totally peaceful. The tears rolled very slowly down Jean's cheeks, she understood. The tranquility of our surroundings remained undisturbed. After a while she said "I am resting behind a rock."

"Yes" I replied.

Often after operations people need to remember that the spirit is lower, partly due to the effects of the anaesthetic and partly due to loss. If part of your body is gone, if your body is no longer complete, then a grieving will follow. It is the natural order of things.

Our spirits are usually recoverable but like the warriors of old we need a time to rest and find strength.

Do you give yourself time behind a rock, a precious capsule of time in which to rebuild before returning to the hectic flow of life? Resting behind a rock need not cost a lot in terms of money, effort or time, it can be so simple.

Sometimes we need someone to show us empathy, to understand. A conscientious person like the soldier of old may need permission to rest in order to return.

Resting behind a rock may take many forms. The walk with the dog hitherto seen as a chore can be approached as a special time to be alone to think our own personal thoughts.

Ten minutes in the midst of a hectic day spent listening to a favourite piece of music, the ironing will wait. If you doubt this look in the ironing basket! Try reclining your seat in the car letting the music from a favourite tape wash over you, no one else in the car park will mind. Yes, they may notice you but will, nevertheless, get on with their lives, and you will still make it to your two o'clock meeting.

The motorway is packed, the warning light flashes to drop your speed to 60mph, why not take the next exit and rest for a while. It may mean that to your family you become a more even tempered commuter, possibly you arrive a little later but the quality of time for them may be better than it was before.

The choices we make are important, they may also be never ending. A person with a limited view may say I have no choice, whilst someone with a deeper insight may say I chose to take that particular option, it wasn't easy, it wouldn't have been what I wanted but in the circumstances it was the only thing that I could do.

The second person is really saying they had a choice to do something that was irksome or difficult but the choice was still there.

If we believe ourselves to have a limited range of choices then that limitation will become our own.

Often during a counselling session I ask people what they would do and in what way they would change their life or situation if they had the power of being magical, if they could pick up a magic wand like a fairy in a Christmas pantomime and make something right. They usually smile, think for a while, and then give a very practical change that they would want to bring about.

Towards the end of the counselling they realise that they have brought about the change, that the magic was their own. It resided inside themselves, they did not need a fairy's wand to make it happen.

This sort of magic is often about choices. It is about refusing to accept limitations which stunt the growth of the spirit and cloud the outlook.

Extraordinary people usually make choices, not always an easy task, however the choices they make no matter what the cost can well contribute to the fact that they are extraordinary.

When he became aware of

his unhappiness

and of his being in the past

He returned to the present

moment

And he was happy

Spencer Johnson, M.D.

Oliver

A simple brooch, six green pieces of glass of varying shades. A present from Oliver. No in-depth look at perception could be complete without a mention of Oliver.

Oliver and I fell in love at first sight mainly because he had such a striking resemblance to my then recently deceased maternal grandfather. He was small, rather as I imagined a leprechaun to be. He grinned, smiled constantly, rubbing his hands together as though enjoying an inner joke.

It was my first day in a new job in a large psychiatric hospital. Oliver informed me when I found him waiting outside my new office that he would be keeping an eye on me and keeping my office clean. He explained where he slept and on which ward he lived. He gave me the name of the charge nurse together with a telephone number. As we had met briefly before I was pleased to know that I would be in his capable care. During that first day he helped me so much. There was furniture to rearrange, requisitions to write and a need for the brewing of numerous cups of tea. Oliver knew so much about the hospital. He had so many stories to tell.

Inside my inherited cupboard we found a couple of beakers somewhat the worse for wear. After much scrutiny, pursing of lips and frowning, Oliver filled them to the brim with what Terry Wogan would call 'builders' tea. It was simply delicious. Sitting there talking to Oliver I couldn't wait to get my suite of offices straight and begin my new work.

At the end of that first day, tired and weary, I turned off the lights and locked the office door.

"Oliver, you will be late for tea on the ward" I said. "I'd best come with you and explain — oh and I must remember to bring more cups in from home tomorrow."

"Why?" queried Oliver.

"So that we can give all our visotors a cup of tea" I replied.

"How many?" asked Oliver.

"Dozens" I laughed, "simply dozens."

It was just a silly throwaway comment, all said at the end of a very busy day.

That night having made tea for my children I slept like the proverbial top. I have often wondered why we use that phrase 'slept like a top' when tops are forever whizzing round and looking colourful! However, the next morning I was up bright and early ready to face the new day. Having set my home to rights, dropped the children at school, I arrived at the main entrance of the hospital. The head porter greeted me with a smile on his face.

"There's a surprise" he said "near your office."

"What kind of a surprise?" I asked.

"You'll see, you'll see."

I opened the door at the bottom of the stairs and suddenly I did see, for on every stair to my office there were cups and cups and more cups. I had never seen so many blue hospital issue cups in my life. As I mounted the stairs I found that whoever had placed them there had left just enough space for me to get up and down the stairs. The rest of each step was covered with cups. Sitting outside my office rubbing his hands together with a lovely gleeful grinning face was Oliver.

"Brought the cups", he said. "For dozens and dozens of people. Now all your visitors can have a cup of tea."

How could I explain to Oliver that I had merely made a throwaway remark.

Having carefully removed himself from his ward, he

had quite religiously visited every ward and every department in the hospital asking them if they had any spare cups that needed returning to the canteen, then having found the cups I was to learn later he had spent hours washing them in a deep sink at the end of his ward. When the charge nurse came on for night duty, he asked him what he was doing with all the cups. He said "I am doing a favour for a new friend, a lady who is having a party and dozens and dozens of people are coming for tea and these are the cups that visitors need." Slowly Oliver and I carried the cups into my office. They filled every desk, every window sill, the coffee table, the mantelpiece, in fact there was not a surface that was not covered with cups, but at least they were less dangerous there than if they had been left on the stairs.

During the course of the day several heads of department, having heard the story of the cups, came in to smile and wish me well. I learned quickly that many people in the world of psychiatry take our words literally just as they are spoken, in much the same way that a child perceives that a parent will tell the truth. Together Oliver and I filled my cupboard with cups and then it was my painful task to explain to him that I had only been joking and that we would not need the rest of the two hundred and fifty cups he had provided. To my horror Oliver stopped grinning, stopped rubbing his hands, sat down on the floor and began to sob. "You don't like me" he said "you don't like my present."

Often in life we think we know the answers not only for ourselves but for other people. We think we are very clever. I didn't feel very clever with Oliver crying on my carpet.

I asked him if he would help me put the other cups together but suddenly this once smiling leprechaun of a man was silent as tears rolled down his face. The catering manager who later became a friend was very kind. He came up from the kitchens with huge trays and on to these he put the cups. He also brought with him a piece of Oliver's favourite gateau because you see this man was much wiser than I. He asked Oliver if the gateau would make up for the cups. Oliver, who had cried by then for over an hour wiped his eyes with the tissues from the box on the table and with a proffered spoon ate his gateau. "You will learn" said the catering manager, "you will learn." He smiled at me knowingly. "Oliver is a lovely man, he will come for you."

Oliver and I continued to love one another and to be friends. One day someone told him it was my birthday. He went to the hospital bank and withdrew a small amount of money. Then with great pomp and circumstance he boarded the bus in the village and travelled into the nearby town. I don't know how much the little green brooch cost him, I only know that it meant a great deal to him to give it to me. It means as much to me today as it did the day he presented me with it. It didn't really matter that it wasn't my birthday and that someone had played a trick upon him, it mattered that he believed it was my birthday and as he presented me not only with the brooch but with a fairy bun with one candle, we sang "Happy Birthday" together and I realised that we can find love in the most unusual and unsuspecting places.

Every time I wear the brooch I think of you Oliver, with your cups upon the stairs and your leprechaun-like movements and I am reminded how very precious love really is.

By the way, Oliver had no idea how he came to be in a psychiatric hospital. He had been there so long that his original records were incomplete with many parts lost or missing. He could only tell me that when he had come there as a young man he had been very fit and it had taken many attendants to hold him down when he was fighting. He remembered a mother and a father who had died and a grandmother who disliked him. He remembered walking the streets and coming to a brick wall and being brought to this place. "This is my home now" he used to say. "How old are you Oliver?" "I think I am in my seventies". At least that was true for his date of birth was there in what remained of his records for all to see. He had been in the Institution for sixty years and he wanted to provide enough cups for everyone at our party to have a drink of tea! He wanted a party. He wanted to help. He looked after me for several years with much love and affection. My relationship with him was very humbling in that he gave so much, expecting so very little in return.

Try how the life of the good
man suits thee,
The life of him who is satisfied
with his
Portion out of the whole, and
satisfied with his own just
Acts and benevolent disposition

Marcus Aurelius, Roman Emperor

Softly, Softly, Catchee Monkey!

Ever since I can remember I have enjoyed reading stories. Stories are like birds on whose wings we sit as we soar to other places and other times. During my life I have been very fortunate in that I have met so many interesting people, people who aroused in me the whole gamut of feelings and responses. The years I spent working in a psychiatric hospital provided one of the deepest learning experiences of my whole life. It was during that time that I was told a story, a story that I had never heard before. Let me take you on a journey.

The hospital was situated miles from the town centre and lay within an expanse of beautiful farmland as all asylums originally were, so as not to cause offence to 'respectable' people. The hospital was at that time over a hundred years old and housed two and half thousand patients.

One day whilst I was driving home through the grounds to the rear entrance of the hospital, I saw a man standing in a field with his arms outstretched. I thought at first that he was a scarecrow then realised that I had never seen a scarecrow in that particular field before. I drove on and went to my home. As usual I made the evening meal for my family but the image of the scarecrow in the field would not leave me. The next morning whilst driving back to work I stopped the car and looked over the hedge but the field was empty.

During the day I used the road two or three times, and the field continued to be just a field. Evening came, nothing there.

Days passed and eventually I forgot about the scarecrow or the man. A few weeks later I stopped the car, parking it carefully as far into the hedge as I safely could. It was blackberry time. On the back seat I had a plastic box and getting out of the car I began to pick the rich ripe fruit. Coming to a gap in the hedge I glanced up and there to my amazement once again I saw the scarecrow. I could see quite clearly now that it was really not a scarecrow, it was a man, it was one of the patients standing in the field with his arms outstretched. I walked along the hedge until I found a gap big enough for me to squeeze through, then I walked across the field to the man with the out-stretched arms. He was not in a trance although he stood very quietly and very very still. I spoke to him, there was no response, but, he smiled and blinked his eyes several times. I looked at his arms and wondered how long he had been holding them at shoulder height away from his body.

"Are you tired?" I asked.

There was no reply.

"Would you like a drink, I live fairly near, I could get you a drink?"

No reply.

"Which ward do you sleep on?"

Gruffly he gave me the number of his ward.

"What is your name?"

"George."

And still he stood arms akimbo.

"Well George" I said "I'd best leave you, you obviously know what you are doing and I am in the middle of picking blackberries."

One word, just one word escaped.

"Jam."

"Oh yes" I said "I am going to make some jam."

"I like jam" he said.

"Well" I said, "when I have made the jam I will bring a pot to the ward for you, I have to hope that this time it turns out right, sometimes it's too thick and sometimes it's too thin."

"Doesn't matter" said George and still he held his arms in this strange position.

As I walked away from George my heart ached for him. Once again the image would not leave me. I couldn't keep my mind on either my music or the television, it was with George. The next day I took a few hours off. I made the jam and having put it into jars I topped it with circles of brightly coloured gingham material. Though it was still warm I decided to take a pot to George on his ward. When I arrived the charge nurse told me that George was usually out walking but said if I was lucky I might find him on the corridor downstairs on his way out. George was there. I presented him with the jam, cooler now. He held the jar in his hands and sniffed at the gingham cover.

"Thank you" he said.

"Field."

"Are you going to the field, George?"

"Yes, field."

I had a busy afternoon. I couldn't stay any longer

with George and after all we both had a lot to do. He was going to the field, and I to the wards. As I drove home later that day there he was, arms outstretched in the same place in the field. I made the tea, I washed up, I did all the things that I needed to do. As I was getting the children ready for bed, I talked to them about George and the way he stood in the field with his arms outstretched.

The next day I went to see George on the ward and asked him if he would like a lift up the road to the field.

"No" he said "walk."

"May I walk with you?"

He grunted.

We walked together. When we reached the field I asked him why his arms were never tired.

"Waiting" he said.

So I stood with George and I waited. I outstretched my arms with his. My arms grew tired within seconds and fell to my side whilst his remained out-stretched.

"I am no use at this" I said.

"Time" said George. "Takes time."

So I went back every day and George taught me that if I persevered I could hold my arms outstretched for quite some time. Eventually as weeks passed, the winter was approaching and the days grew colder.

"What will you do when it's very cold? It will be too cold to stand out here" I said.

George, with whom I had no eye contact whatso-ever, put down his arms and looked at his feet.

"Sad" he said.

"Do you ever stand like that on the ward?" I said.

For the first time he looked at me, his eyes full of reproach. He must have thought that I was an ignorant stupid individual. For in that look I saw the answer. Of course he couldn't stand like that on the ward, he would have only brought about an increase in his medication, a controlling increase, words in his records to suggest that he was mad.

One day in late autumn George and I sat in the field on a plastic mac taken from the boot of my car.

"Why George? Why? is it for peace, is it for quiet, is it for self discipline, or do you do it for a sense of freedom?"

He smiled.

"A man" said George, "wanted to catch monkeys, lots of men wanted to catch monkeys in the jungle."

There were long pauses as he continued the story.

"Every man came back, first man two monkeys, second man three monkeys, third man no monkeys, no monkeys to sell. Then a wise man came to teach them how to catch monkeys. He took them into the jungle and stood very still with his arms out like this."

George jumped up and stretched his arms out.

"Soon many monkeys came, sat on his head, on his shoulders, on his arms. He stood very very still, then he catched all the monkeys. Softly, softly, catchee monkee."

George and I sat on the plastic mac for quite some time without speaking. I felt too humble to say anything. Later I was to wonder why I didn't know the story of the monkey man, why I had never known it. I who was supposed to be so well read had none of that wisdom. The rain came, great fat blobs. In no time at all we were sitting underneath the plastic mac with it above our heads, the raindrops fell upon us making soft plopping noises. George liked the noise. He had never had a plastic mac and had never ever sat under a plastic mac with anyone let alone a woman! Slowly it grew dark and reluctantly it was necessary for us to make our way to our respective beds.

"I liked your story George" I said. "I will have to learn how to stand."

"Takes time" said George.

He was right, it does take time. It took me months and months to master the art of standing with my arms outstretched, turning off my mind so that it blocked out the pain of actually holding out my arms without support. When I had achieved it I felt as though I had really learned something. No, I realise I will not go into a jungle to catch monkeys but every time I am in a discussion or a debate I remember George and the story of the monkey man and I try hard to listen so that softly, softly, I can catchee monkee. Thank you George, thank you for teaching me, thank you for letting me pass this on. I don't know where you are now, probably long gone, but your spirit lives on in this particular section of this particular book.

Often we find ourselves in situations where we are ready to retort. The result of this is that often we find ourselves prematurely catapulted into an argumentative situation. It uses up our energy robbing us of vitality, a wasted period of time. The art of listening is important, the monkey man standing in the jungle needed to listen, to concentrate, to take it all in.

George standing in the field listened to every bird, every car on the lane, every football, every rabbit, every passing creature and said nothing, he just took it all in.

The capacity to listen, absorb and take in what other people say without immediately responding is not only a gift but a discipline. Once achieved it saves an awful lot of energy and wasted effort.

Just for the sheer hell of it, next time you are out in the country or standing in your garden on an early summer morning when everyone else is probably in bed, why not try standing very still then lift up your arms to shoulder height at either side of you, switch off your mind, imagine that you can do it. Once you can do it you will enjoy it. Breathe deeply, enjoy the air, stare ahead taking in the view and if there isn't a distant view then focus your attention on a plant in your garden at eye level. Say to yourself I can do this, I can be in control of at least part of myself, part of the time.

It's alright if you only manage two minutes, one minute, half a minute, what does it matter — you made the effort anyway. Sometimes in a personal situation you will need to keep quiet for much longer than half a minute, containing yourself and your emotions because at that moment the other person will need to be more important than yourself. The discipline has to start somewhere, go on give it a try, middle of a field, top of a hill, bottom of your garden, wherever doesn't really matter.

P.77.

P.81

holistic touch yoga

Aughton WI hut.

*Let it not be in any man's
power to say
Truly of thee that thou art
not simple.*

Marcus Aurelius

Billy

Billy spent his days with his head bowed, gaze averted, sweeping the corridors of the psychiatric hospital which had been his home for many years. Billy was a mute; at least, that's what everyone believed; that's what he wanted them to believe. But patients are not always what they seem.

This is the story of Billy. I met him 13 years ago in a large psychiatric hospital. I had applied for a senior post and after being short-listed was called for interview in the company of seven other people. One of the senior nursing staff was given the task of taking us on a tour of the hospital. We walked from ward to ward, department to department; the day seemed endless. Our guide talked incessantly, most of the time about the history of psychiatry and the well-being of patients, and the way in which the care of such patients had changed over the years, so that psychiatry could no longer be classed as the Cinderella of the service.

After some hours, we came to a large, long, drab, empty corridor; there were doors all the way along one side, and standing in the middle of the emptiness was an elderly man with sweeping brush in hand. His head was tucked well down and he appeared to be looking intently at particles of dust beneath the bristles of his brush.

As we approached he seemed not to notice us at all and went on diligently sweeping and sweeping, always in the same place. I looked at him for some considerable time, but he made no attempt whatsoever to raise his head or to answer my gaze. On seeing me doing this, our guide said quite cheerily: "This is Billy; Billy's very happy here with us, aren't you Billy?"

He patted Billy on the head as though he was a small child. No further words were said as we walked down the corridor. By then the guide was talking incessantly once more.

I looked back, and, over my shoulder saw Billy watching us. The senior nurse looked at me and said:

"Don't worry about Billy, Billy is mute, he hasn't spoken for over 20 years; he is one of those people who is very contented with his lot."

As the tour continued, I wondered if our guide knew Billy intimately. Did he spend hours talking to him? Did he really know?

Some weeks later, having received a letter telling me that the post was mine, I started work. It seemed that every day I would pass down that same drab corridor, and Billy would be there sweeping. Every time I passed Billy, I spoke to him.

"Good morning, Billy; Good afternoon, Billy; how are you, Billy?" There was never a response.

Days turned into weeks, weeks into months, I enjoyed my work. It seemed amazing to me that I could be paid for a job in which almost every minute was enjoyable.

I have always believed that it is impossible to measure with any certainty the true response of another human being, and because of this Billy became a challenge. I would sit on the window-sill close to him, chattering away as though we were having a two-way conversation. Billy swept on as though I wasn't there at all.

But one day a remarkable thing happened. It was to change my relationship with Billy. As I was leaving the house, the postman handed me some letters. I hastily popped them into my bag and took them to work with me, and on arrival opened them together with the department mail. Unfortunately, one of the letters contained some bad news. I was to report immediately to another hospital to undergo a rather serious operation. I had known for some time that this operation might be necessary, but suddenly to realise that I was summoned, as it were, immediately, was quite daunting.

I called in my staff and explained that I would be away for at least three months, and that we must spend the day trying to get things in order. This we did for a couple of hours, and then feeling rather glum, I decided to visit one of the geriatric wards, as this always seemed to cheer me up. I passed down the corridor as usual, visited the old ladies, and then on my way back to the office, I passed Billy. As I passed close to him, his hand came out and touched mine. For the very first time, I found myself looking into his blue, blue eyes. As soon as I looked at him, he looked away, withdrew his arm from mine, and mumbled:

"You didn't speak! you didn't speak to me today."

I was so surprised, that I wondered as I looked at

Billy's head once more bowed down, as he intently brushed the dust at his feet, if, in fact, I had dreamt that he had spoken and touched me. One or two people passed up the corridor, and Billy said no more, but when we were once more alone, I touched his arm and said:

"Billy, you can speak, you can really speak Billy."

He nodded his head and drew me to the side of the corridor, and carefully opening one of the doors, beckoned to me to follow him inside. I did so.

"Something is wrong," he said, without looking at me at all. "Something is wrong with you today."

"Yes." I said. "I'm going into hospital."

"I knew there was something wrong, I always know."

"Billy." I said, "Why is it that everyone thinks that you are mute?"

"That's a long story," said Billy.

"I'm going into hospital, I'm afraid."

"Don't be afraid," said Billy.

"Will you still talk to me when I get back," I said. He shrugged his shoulders, and then I asked:

"Why did you choose to talk to me? Why did you choose today?"

"Today was different," said the old man. "Today you were sad. I can always tell when people are sad by the number of steps they take up the corridor. People walk differently when they are sad. You walked differently today."

"Thank you for speaking to me," I said, "thank you so much."

Billy gave a wry smile.

"That's all right," he replied, "you always speak to me. Everyday — morning Billy; afternoon Billy; night Billy, you always speak."

"Am I worth trusting, Billy?" He shrugged his shoulders again.

"When I come back Billy, please talk to me again."

He pushed me gently through the door but remained in the room, as though he was afraid for both of us to be seen coming out together. I returned to my office, completed my work, went home and prepared for my stay in hospital.

During the weeks that followed, I gave much thought to my conversation with Billy. During the painful times it paled into insignificance, I began to believe it had never happened, and that I had been given to flights of fancy and imaginings. But three months later I was back at work, as chirpy as ever, and on the first day I walked down the corridor and there, as if there had been no span of time in between, stood Billy, brush in hand, sweeping just the same as ever.

I waited until the corridor was quite empty, and then I walked up to him.

"Hello Billy," I said, "I'm back, I'm better, would you like to go for a walk." There was no reply, no look, no glance, no shrugging of the shoulders, no lifting of the head, nothing.

Everything was just as it had been, the first time we had ever met.

"Oh Billy," I said, "Oh Billy," and then Billy said quietly:

"I'd like to go out, just for a walk."

A few days later, with the charge nurse's permission, Billy and I went walking in the grounds. The charge nurse was very glad, he said, that someone was taking an interest in Billy, for Billy had noone who cared for him at all, apart from the staff, who liked him because he was quiet. It was they who brought him presents at Christmas, and on his birthday, it was they, the nurses, who made arrangements for his birthday cake, it was they who tried to make the ward like home.

We walked around the grounds, and then as we came to a deserted track, Billy asked:

"You've got a car?"

"Yes" I replied.

"I'd like to go out please."

So the following week, Billy and I went out for a drive, and it was on the banks of a nearby river that Billy told me his story and explained to me why he had decided to be mute.

It is not a pleasant story, it belongs far back in time. It belongs in the twenties, in what was the old asylum.

It belongs in a ward with 130 beds, and a foot of space between each one, because it was to this environment that Billy was admitted.

He had little knowledge or memory of his life before that, other than that he had been a teacher and lived at home with his mother and father, and then he commented:

"I think I had what they call a breakdown, and one day I was here. There was a lot of noise in the ward — a great deal of noise; shouting, shuffling, banging, screaming. It seemed to me that it was all noise, all terrible, terrible noise."

In those days, apparently, there were no trained nurses, only attendants who, for very small wages, looked after the inmates.

Billy had been in the ward for a very short time, when a large, burly male attendant approached him.

"Hello Jones," said the attendant. "What football team do you support?" Billy remembered that he smiled and said "Blackburn Rovers."

"Oh dear," frowned the attendant, and Billy found himself dragged away and placed in a most terrible, terrible room.

"I knew afterwards what it was called," he said, "The Pads."

Even now, in the warm sunlight, sitting on the banks of the river, a picnic lunch between us, even here with all the security and warmth, Billy obviously felt fear, saying "The Pads". "I hated it," he said, "I was sure I would die."

Eventually the door was opened and Billy was taken out. He was given a drink and then after about an hour, the attendant approached him again.

"Which football team do you support," he said.

"Blackburn Rovers," said Billy, and then it was once more, the terrible, terrible room. Sitting on the river bank, Billy's words did not come easily, they came with effort, with stuttering, great pauses.

Billy wasn't sure how long he spent in the padded cell at that time, but when he came out, another man appeared to be in charge, and he led Billy away, away from the padded cell.

Billy looked around the ward; he felt hurt and confused. Trying to escape from the noise, he looked for a quiet corner and then he saw a man sitting on a bed at the far end of the ward. On his bed were five withered brown leaves, for it was autumn, and the man was touching the leaves, with great reverence. Billy went over to him.

"What football team do you support," he said to the man.

The man smiled, without looking at Billy — an empty smile. "Queens Park Rangers," he replied.

"Thank you," said Billy. After that, life became easier for Billy. The next day when he was asked about his football preferences, he named the right team.

"Good on you," smiled the burly attendant. "You've learnt the rules already," and he patted Billy heartedly on the back.

"It was really then," explained Billy, "that I decided, it was a very strange world that I'd entered and that if I were mad, this place was about a kind of madness, much more mad than I."

He endured the life that the asylum had to offer for some years, and then one day, could endure it no longer.

"It was then I decided not to speak," he said. There were tears running down his face, I took out a tissue, and wiped them away.

"Have you had enough talking for one day, Billy?" I asked. He nodded. "Do you ever talk to anyone?"

"Yes" he replied. "I talk to the cats, they're all over the grounds you know, dozens of them. I talk to the birds and I talk to one or two of the patients, the ones that everyone thinks are very, very mad. It's all right to talk to them, you see, because if they said that I could speak, no one would believe them; we are all just patients."

Billy and I spent many many hours together. Billy knew everything there was to know about hospital life; he knew where everything was kept, he knew which members of the staff loved other members of the staff, which husband was meeting whose wife, he knew when the consultant was late on his rounds, and he knew the staff who arrived late in the morning. He noticed if they had hangovers, but he noticed most the staff who really cared.

He told me of one nurse, who always gave him extra sugar in his tea, because she said: "As you don't talk, Billy, I don't know how much sugar you take. But the sugar will do you good and give you energy." Billy liked her. He liked, too, those members of staff who, as he said, "kept themselves smart. That's how nurses should look."

I asked Billy if I could write about him, if I could tell his story. At first he said:

"No — no I wouldn't like that." But then he decided "In 10 years I will be very old or dead, and if you want to tell my story then, you can. No one will listen, Vera; no one really cares."

There isn't a lot I can say, now, about Billy. His story is told. What strides have been made in psychiatry? There are now psychotropic drugs and deep in-group therapy, to say nothing of psycho-analysis, home-leave and rehabilitation. Group homes in the community flourish and elderly disturbed people strive to make new lives in the community. But for the Billys of this world, all this progress, this futuristic look at what mental illness is about, is too late. For they remember the years of suffering, of misunderstanding, of ignorance, but in Billy's case, they were also years of ingenuity, of using a mind that had always been bright, to its best purpose.

Billy, who at a very early age could read and write, had in fact been to university and obtained a degree; he was a clever man, who found himself in an unfriendly climate. But he, with his brightness of spirit, took out his survival kit and used it. We praise great explorers, who conquer nature, who achieve great things. But to my mind, Billy is one of the greatest of them all, for he explored a facet of human nature and behaviour, that perhaps no one hitherto had seen. He became mute by choice. He chose to whom he would speak. Not for him the social hypocrisy of life. For him only the pain of truth.

During our last conversation Billy said:

"It's safe to talk to some people, because they have love in their faces and dangerous to talk to others, because there is only hardness there."

Billy taught me so much. He made me feel humble. He had so many answers, so much perception, so much insight into the human condition. But most of all he had so much courage. He made his choices and lived by them — he managed to survive.

During the time I spent working in psychiatry I was privileged to meet Oliver, Billy and George. Each of these men had spent over 35 years as patients in a large psychiatric hospital.

Into my life they not only brought wisdom but a deeper knowledge of the meaning of the word survival. I am humbled by their dignity.

Afterword

The book is finished. I have tried to talk to you through its pages and now we have the Afterword. Once I was asked 'why bother with an Afterword?' Trying hard to find a bright and intelligent answer is difficult. Then I realised that the reason the Afterword is written is to gather all the strands of stories and thoughts together and that is my reason for its presence.

As I write, the River Leven flows by. Sitting on a bench this sunny spring day is like heaven to me. A life bonus, a deposit in my own emotional bank. A large deposit at that! Worries about water shortages seem far away as this river flows on as it has flowed for decades.

The little celandines are opening their bright eyes beneath the trees whilst a worried thrush becomes agitated at my approach.

Four young ducks waddle up the slippery muddy bank towards me, then on looking at me from a safe distance three of them rise as one, flap their wings and land with a great whoosh back on the water. Not so the one remaining duck. This mallard takes a chance and stays put. Weighing me up. Then when he is ready he too takes off, flying to join his peers who by now seem far away from the perceived danger zone. Their behaviour reminds me of people. The bravest of us do not always go with the flow, holding back to make our own decisions in life.

Gracefully a white swan proceeds up river then stops and with a further graceful movement rests a long, elegant, yet obviously weary neck on the pure white feathered breast, reminding me that we all need respite at some time in life.

So many people have never ever had the chance to look at and appreciate nature. Have never for so many many reasons been helped or encouraged to understand the patterns of life. Despite death, jilting, joy and happiness, despite earthquake and flood, the pattern of nature continues. Never have I liked the autumn months despite the beautiful colours, tones and hues. Autumn is not for me. Is it because I dread the long winter months when growth seems to be held in suspense? For me this season, spring, is the best, full of hope and promise. The flowers in bud, the birds returning from warmer climes. Everything begins to have possibilities and I feel positive to the point of being joyful. I hope this book has stirred so many emotions within you that it leaves you with the feelings of spring, with joy and promise. Tied together firmly with a ribbon of hope. Wonderful encouraging hope. For life does go on and nature's clock continues to tick no matter what.

Long after we quit this mortal coil the celandines will bloom and thrushes, to say nothing of swans, will go about their business. For life is eternal, death being merely a punctuation mark to indicate a change of pattern.

God Bless.

Like yourself and try to be happy. Our life on earth is important, you are a unique individual, your contribution to the human race and our society is invaluable.

When one door of happiness closes, another opens; but often we look so long at the closed door that we do not see the one which has been opened for us

Helen Keller